Black & White QUILTS
by Design

Kay M. Capps CROSS

American Quilter's Society

P. O. Box 3290 • Paducah, KY 42002-3290
www.AmericanQuilter.com

Located in Paducah, Kentucky, the American Quilter's Society (AQS) is dedicated to promoting the accomplishments of today's quilters. Through its publications and events, AQS strives to honor today's quiltmakers and their work and to inspire future creativity and innovation in quiltmaking.

Editor: Toni Toomey
Copy Editor: Chrystal Abhalter
Graphic Design: Amy Chase
Cover Design: Michael Buckingham
Quilt Photos: Charles R. Lynch
How-to-Photos: Kay M. Capps Cross

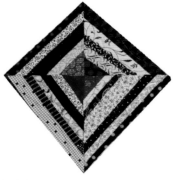

Library of Congress Cataloging-in-Publication Data

Cross, Kay M. Capps.
  Black & white quilts by design / by Kay M. Capps Cross.
    p. cm.
  Includes bibliographical references and index.
  ISBN 1-57432-904-9
    1. Patchwork--Patterns. 2. Quilting--Patterns. 3. Black in art.
  4. White in art. I. Title.
  TT835.C74895 2006
  746.46'041--dc22

                              2006008496

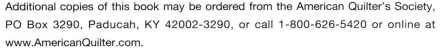

Additional copies of this book may be ordered from the American Quilter's Society, PO Box 3290, Paducah, KY 42002-3290, or call 1-800-626-5420 or online at www.AmericanQuilter.com.

Proudly printed and bound in the
United States of America

DEDICATION

To my Grandma Hap for always asking,
encouraging, loving, and helping.
To my Grandma Mimi because she was
always glad to.

ACKNOWLEDGMENTS

I would like to thank:

the folks at AQS for allowing me to take this wonderful journey. Toni, you are insightful, inspiring, encouraging, patient, and really funny.

the Fab Four for their continual encouragement and support,

my quilt teachers for inspiring and shaping my personal style,

my quilt students and pattern testers for coming back for more and helping me hone my skills,

my new quilt friends for welcoming me in this exciting adventure,

my grandmother for binding circles around me and my quilts,

my financial and emotional backers (parents and siblings are just the best things),

my children for being the fire and light in my life,

and my He-man for doing the laundry, the cooking, the dishes, the mowing, and dragging home a slab of beef to the cave while I wrote this book.

CONTENTS

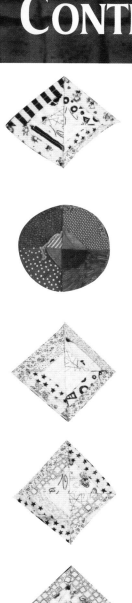

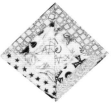

INTRODUCTION

So often in our quilt making, we get caught up in what color would look right here and what color would be best there. We also worry about a color combination matching the recipient's home decorating scheme. Well, let's throw our worries out the window because none of those things matter in this book!

My journey into black-and-white fabrics began at a very black-and-white time in my life. I was not seeing a lot of gray or color. While making quilts in this palette, I felt my creativity break free. Gradually, color crept back into my life and my designs. Color has continued to tweak my designs with just a touch of *pazowie*. That little spot of brilliance on the black-and-white palette can be so explosive and beautiful. My hope is that you will share this creative explosion with me and maybe learn a little bit as we dabble and play in black and white. I expect you will be as thrilled by the beauty of your creations as I am to bring these designs to you.

Don't get me wrong, I thoroughly enjoy color but I really thrive on the challenge of creating quilts with only black-and-white with a small splash of color. We are going to journey through the black-and-white world of value and contrast to create some awesome quilts. The graphic and angular patterns will give your mind a rest from color questions and allow you to concentrate on contrast as the basic building block in these simple yet effective designs.

While black-and-white fabrics have been tricky to find in the past, I have found the search to be fun and fruitful. There are many more choices out there now. Even though the selection of black-and-white fabrics grows, the hunt continues to be exhilarating. There is always that elusive piece with just the right scale, the right print, or even the right value that needs to be found.

The visual strength of contrast in quilting is the same whether it is clearly stated in black and white or presented more subtly in shades of color. Hopefully this book will be the start of a wonderful journey for you. One of the really fun things about this book is that you can apply what we learn to all of your subsequent quilting adventures. I enjoy teaching and using the stress-free quilting methods I present in this book. I had such fun creating these pieces that I am eager to share them with you. So please, enough chit-chat—let's get quilting.

TOOLS, MATERIALS, AND TECHNIQUES

We all have our favorite tools and techniques in our quilting. I will share some tools and materials that have been helpful to me along the way, and some techniques to help you successfully complete the projects in this book.

Tools and Materials

Rotary-cutting equipment

Rotary cutter with a sharp blade

Start your cutting sessions with a sharp rotary blade. This one small item will improve your accuracy and speed tremendously.

Acrylic ruler

Whichever ruler you use, be consistent throughout quilt projects. Changing rulers (brands) midstream can affect your results.

Add-A-Quarter Ruler™

This ruler (fig. 1) is a great help trimming ¼" seam allowances. It makes foundation piecing a breeze. If you like neat and tidy seam allowances, this ruler is for you.

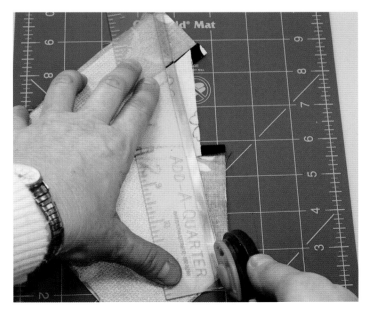

Fig. 1. Add-A-Quarter ruler

Foundation piecing materials

Sulky® Soft 'n Sheer™

I don't use paper for foundation piecing because I don't care for the way tearing away the paper distresses the stitches. All that tearing is also a lot of work. The secret to my foundation piecing is Soft 'n Sheer, a permanent, stabilizer used in machine embroidery (fig. 2).

Though it was never intended to be used in quilting, I find this lightweight, non-woven nylon the perfect foundation fabric. It is tough enough to withstand some unsewing, yet supple enough to leave in my quilts. It adds body that I think enhances the quilt.

Fig. 2. This lightweight, permanent stabilizer is the perfect fabric for foundation piecing.

Sulky® Iron-On Transfer Pen

I use an iron-on transfer pen when I need to make multiple copies of a foundation pattern. I trace a pattern onto plain white paper once, and then iron the pattern onto as many pieces of foundation fabric as I need for an entire quilt.

Techniques

Foundation piecing

I do everything I can to take the work out of foundation piecing. I like to work with precut strips, not big hunks of fabric.

Here is a brief overview of how I foundation piece:

1. Trace or iron transfer the pattern onto your foundation fabric.
2. If needed, add the numbers on the pattern to the foundation to aid in piecing. Do not put numbers in sections that will be covered by a light fabric. They may show through your finished quilt.
3. Always make sure a strip is large enough to cover the section of the pattern with a ¼" seam allowance all around before sewing it to the foundation fabric.
4. To sew the first two strips to your foundation fabric, select the appropriate fabric strips for pieces 1 and 2. Then with right sides together, position the two strips to the *wrong side* of the foundation fabric along the first seam line (fig. 3).

Fig. 3. Position strips along the first seam line.

5. Hold the pieces up to the light to make sure that section 1 is completely covered, with a ¼" seam allowance all around. Then with the foundation fabric right side up, sew along the stitching line.

Angled seams made easy

When you have an angled stitching line, it can be tricky to position your strips correctly. If you start with a clean ¼" seam allowance, you will be way ahead of the game. I call it "pretrimming."

1. Sew the strips to the foundation along the seam line stitched with red thread (fig. 4). Flip the black strip back, and finger press.

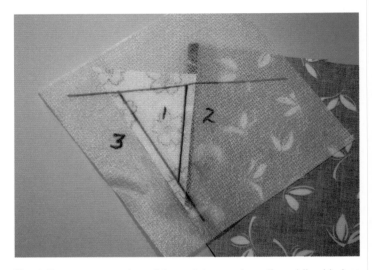

Fig. 4. The seam sewn in red thread shows where the white strip has been added to the foundation.

2. Locate the angled seam line that you will be stitching. In this case, the stitching line is between sections 1 and 3. Fold back the foundation along the target stitching line and trim away excess fabric to create a ¼" seam allowance (fig. 5, page 9).
3. Flip the foundation fabric back in place. Align the next strip with the pretrimmed edge and sew along the angled stitching line (fig. 6, page 9).

Pretrimming with scissors

Sometimes, in tight spots, it can be cumbersome and difficult to pretrim the seam allowance with a rotary cutter. It is easier to cut it with the scissors to keep everything lined up. You may simply prefer doing all of your pretrimming with scissors. Whether you use scissors or a rotary cutter, trimming those ¼"

seam allowances in advance makes it easier to get all of your fabrics lined up before sewing.

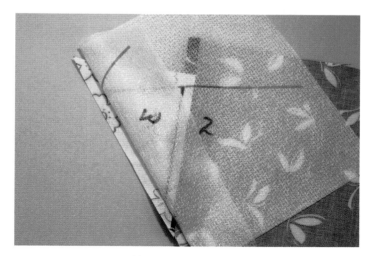

Fig. 5. Trim to create a ¼" seam allowance.

Fig. 6. The new angled seam line is shown with red thread.

1. Position the block with the foundation side up and locate the next stitching line. Lay the strip you are adding right side down over the section it needs to cover.

2. Flip the edge of the strip back to expose the stitching line that you will be sewing (fig. 7). Finger press the strip on the stitching line.

Fig. 7. Finger press the strip along the stitching line.

3. Cut away the excess ¼" from the finger-pressed crease (fig. 8). Now it is easy to position your strip with the precut seam allowance.

4. Position the strip right sides together under the previously sewn strip, aligning the crease with the stitching line on the foundation fabric. Check the position by holding the pieces up to the light, and then stitch with confidence.

Fig. 8. Trim the strip to create the ¼" seam allowance.

VALUE, SCALE, AND ZINGERS

Since this is a book about black-and-white quilts, we don't need to concern ourselves with any color questions until the tail end of the fabric selection process. That is where zingers come in. Without the color question as a basic element in fabric selection, we need to focus on value and scale to give our quilts interest and movement. Too many fabrics of the same value or scale can produce murky quilts without definition. It takes practice to make fabric choices that accentuate the crispness of a design. Let's take a closer look at value.

Value

Value is the lightness or darkness of a color. In quilting it is the lightness or darkness of a fabric. In this book, it is the lightness or darkness of black-and-white prints. In the lists of materials needed for each quilt in this book, the fabrics are described in five values from lightest to darkest (fig. 1).

Fig. 1. Black-and-white fabrics in five values

Value is not a simple "black-and-white" issue. There is great importance to the *relative* value of fabrics. The same fabric, used with different combinations, can have very different values. Look at the samples in figure 2 to see relative value at work. Relative to the other fabrics in the set, the light fabric in set 1 is

the medium-light fabric in set 2, and the medium fabric in set 3.

Dark	Medium Dark	Medium	Medium Light	Light

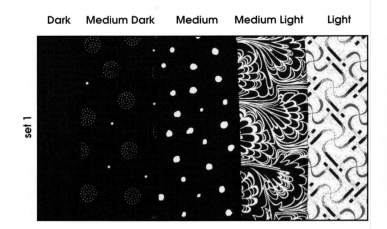

set 1

set 2

set 3

Fig. 2. A fabric's relative value depends on the other fabrics in the set.

It is easier than you might think to see value differences between fabrics with the naked eye. The trick is to lay the fabrics side-by-side and squint while you look at them. If you squint hard enough, the only differences you will be able to see between the fabrics are their values. (This works equally well with colored fabrics.)

Scale

Scale is the size of the pattern on a fabric. Scale plays a part in determining value, but it also makes a major contribution to the design clarity of a quilt. Remembering that there can be many steps in between, we will break scale down into three broad tiers (figs. 3–5).

Whether a quilt has many fabrics or just a few, if it has too many fabrics of the same scale it will be flat and lifeless. With all fabrics in a similar scale, like the ones in figure 6 (page 12), a quilt will become confusing and uninteresting. There need to be scale differences to allow a quilt to dance and sparkle. Variations in scale give our eyes something to focus on and travel to.

Fig. 4. Medium-scale prints

Fig. 3. Small-scale prints

Fig. 5. Large-scale prints

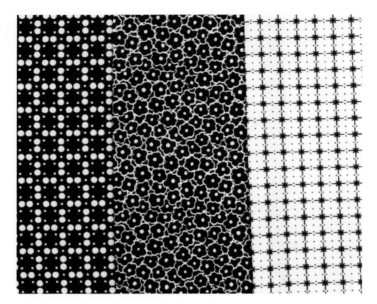

Fig. 6. Without variations in scale, the different values are not enough to bring this set of fabrics to life.

Fig. 7. Mix up the scale, and look what you get!

Zingers

You can use value and scale to liven up a black-and-white quilt. One other element that really brings them to life is the zinger. Your zinger fabric adds a spark of color that pops out from all the black and white. Scale and value differences in the black-and-white fabrics make these quilts dance, but the zingers make them sing.

The zinger needs to be a rich, intense, clear color.

Let's look at the two red fabrics in figure 8. They are both beautiful, but one is a hands-down winner for a zinger. The first red really pops out from the black-and-white fabrics, while the murkier, toned-down red is flat. Look how the white is whiter and the black is deeper against the clear pure red of the first fabric. Zingers can be tone-on-tone fabrics or have some pattern, as long as it doesn't dilute the intensity of the zinger color. Any quilt made with these fabrics would be a stunner.

Fig. 8. Use bright, undiluted colors for your zingers.

Naturally, I gravitate toward red as a zinger because it makes the most graphic and classic combination with black and white. I do like to play with other colors, though, and have used green, pink, purple, yellow, and orange to brighten my quilts. Whatever color you choose for your zinger, go for a clear, undiluted color, and let it pop!

SNUGGLETIME, HE-MAN

81" x 99"
Pieced by Sue Elsbernd, Calmar, Iowa. Quilted by the author.

While many of my quilts tend to look contemporary, there are some that celebrate more traditional designs. SNUGGLETIME, HE-MAN is a blend of the traditional Four-Patch and a version of a Prairie Queen block. I gave these simple elements a modern twist with their combination and coloration. Steeped in tradition, this quilt is one of my favorites for its history and its story. It is infused with my life and my love. My marriage is chronicled in each seam and square.

In the quilt, you can see twelve blocks, each surrounded by four blocks encircling and connected to each other. There are two ways to view the tale of these centers. In the man's account, we find my husband standing alone in the center block. Unaccompanied, yet not lonely, he sails his solitary ship while the story flows around him. This man is an island. While his family narrative vines around him, he remains blissfully unaware that he is buoyed on all sides by those that love him. Encircled with his family's love, the man stands alone.

My account presents a different scenario. Place me in the center of the design and I am reveling in the connections of friends and family. I yearn for and seek out attachments in life. They sustain and strengthen me. Much as a life vest, I wrap them around me to keep afloat. I thrill to the warmth of my children's arms enfolding me and am recharged by their natural energy. Life ebbs and flows around the entangled web of our family, and I float with the buoyancy of life's intertwining relationships. Encircled by my family's love, the woman stands encouraged.

And always, I welcome my husband to wrap his strong arms around me—then it's snuggletime, He-man!

Gathering Your Fabrics

The yardages are based on 42" wide fabric.
- Medium-light: black-on-white scroll print, medium scale for the background color and the borders, 7½ yd.
- Dark: white-on-black almost solid black print, tiny scale for the checkerboards, 1⅛ yd.
- Medium-dark: white-on-black fine cobweb print, large scale for the checkerboards, 1⅛ yd.
- Zinger: red tone-on-tone, medium scale, ⅞ yd.
- Backing: 5½ yd.
- Batting: 89" x 107"
- Binding: (bias cut) ⅞ yd.

Fabric Suggestions

Four fabrics with the right values give this quilt its movement and sparkle (figs. 1 and 2).

- Choose a light, cozy print for the block background. Shirtings and light conversation prints work beautifully.
- Make the medium-dark fabric pop. Choose a fabric that definitely contrasts with the dark fabric. Be bold and dramatic with this choice to give the quilt depth.

Fig. 1. Use shirtings or light conversation prints for your light fabric.

Fig. 2. Use dark and medium-dark fabrics that stand out from each other.

- The medium-dark and dark fabrics should be close in value, but not too close. If they are too close in value, the piecing will appear flat instead of textured.
- Choose your binding carefully. When it is well chosen, it makes a bold statement about the care and consideration that went into the quilt. You can use the medium-dark fabric for this.

Making Four-Patch Checkerboards

You will assemble four-patch units into checkerboards that will be placed horizontally and checkerboards that will be placed vertically in the quilt.

1. From the 2" strips, sew 17 medium-light/dark strip-sets, and 17 medium-light/medium-dark strip-sets. Then cut 2" segments from each strip-set (fig. 3).

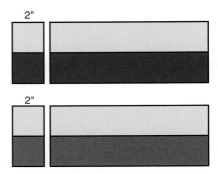

Fig. 3. From strip-sets, cut 329 medium-light/dark segments and 329 medium-light/medium-dark segments.

2. Sew four-patch units with one of each segment, then assemble 51 horizontal checkerboards and 16 vertical checkerboards. In figure 4, notice how

Cutting List	All strips are cut across width of fabric unless otherwise stated. Binding strips are cut on the bias.	
Fabric	**First Cut** (Trim selvages off all strips after first cut.)	**Second Cut**
Medium-light, 7½ yd.	34 strips 2" for checkerboards	
....	35 strips 3½"	62 rectangles 3½" x 9½" for checkerboard sides
....		32 squares 3½" x 3½" for block centers
....	Reserve remaining 3½" strips for inner and outer borders	
....	7 strips 3⅞"	64 squares 3⅞" x 3⅞" for block corners
Medium-dark, 1⅛ yd......	17 strips 2" for checkerboards	
Dark, 1⅛ yd.	17 strips 2" for checkerboards	
Zinger, ⅞ yd.	7 strips 3⅞"	64 squares 3⅞"
....	From excess, cut 4 squares 3½" for border cornerstones	

the top four-patch unit is positioned in the two different checkerboards. Set aside the rest of the four-patch units, 128 to use in the Snuggle blocks.

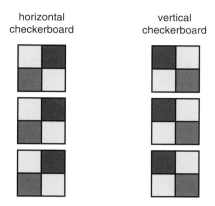

horizontal checkerboard | vertical checkerboard

Fig. 4. Assemble 51 horizontal checkerboards and 16 vertical checkerboards.

3. For the center of the quilt top, use your checkerboards and your 3½" x 9½" medium-light rectangles to assemble 15 horizontal blocks and 16 vertical blocks, as shown in figure 5. Set aside the rest of the checkerboards to use in the pieced border.

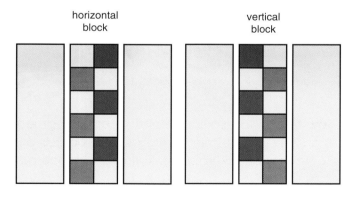

horizontal block | vertical block

Fig. 5. Assemble 15 horizontal blocks and 16 vertical blocks.

Making Snuggle Blocks

1. For the corners of the Snuggle blocks use 3⅞" zinger squares and medium-light 3⅞" squares to make 128 half-square triangles (fig. 6).

Fig. 6. Make 128 half-square triangles.

2. Use corner triangle squares, four-patch units, and your 3½" medium-light squares to assemble 32 Snuggle blocks (fig. 7).

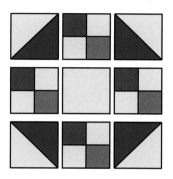

Fig. 7. Assemble 32 Snuggle blocks.

3. Use your Snuggle blocks and horizontal checkerboard blocks to assemble 5 horizontal rows and 4 vertical rows according to the quilt assembly diagram on page 16. Then join the rows as shown.

Adding the Borders

1. For the inner border, join eight 3½" medium-light strips. Cut two 81½" strips and sew one to each side of the quilt. Then cut two 69½" strips and sew them to the top and bottom of the quilt.
2. For the pieced middle border, sew two strips with 9⅔ horizontal checkerboards in each strip. Sew one to each side of the quilt, as shown in the quilt assembly diagram on page 16. Sew two strips with 7⅔ horizontal checkerboards in each one. Add a 3½" zinger square to the end of each strip and sew these to the top and bottom of the quilt.
3. For the outer border, join the remaining 3½" strips. Cut two 93½" strips and sew one to each side of the quilt. Then cut two 81½" strips and sew them to the top and bottom of the quilt.

Finishing Touches

- To enhance the strong lines of this quilt, I stitched in the ditch on the checkerboard piecing. Contrasting that with a little softness, I quilted the background in an allover swirling motif that mimics the pattern in the medium-light and zinger fabrics.

- Be sure to sew a fun, snappy binding on this quilt. Because of the checkerboard borders, the quilt appears to have no borders. This really puts the emphasis on the frame provided by the binding.

- Label the quilt with your own "snuggle" story and be sure you sign it.

  I wish you many happy hours with your accomplishment. Enjoy it!

SNUGGLETIME, HE-MAN quilt assembly

FLANNEL NEWBIES

64½" x 64½" Made by the author.

This quilt came into being for two reasons. First, it was an exercise to conquer my fear of flannel, and second, a fabric wouldn't quit talking to me. I was working in a quilt shop where all these gorgeous flannels kept appearing on the shelves. I was enjoying fondling them, but I certainly wasn't taking them home to make samples. I was scared to death of them! They stretched and gave, and weren't they for PJs after all?

I successfully avoided the flannel aisle for some time. After a while, I started approaching the soft fluffy bolts and moved from fondling to pulling them out and unrolling just a bit of them. That was my undoing. I unrolled one of the bolts and almost had to get a mop to clean up my drool. This fabric was absolutely stunning. From then on, these flannels would not leave me alone. They called greetings to me as I arrived for work and chattered at me all day. I played with them often, but that was not enough. I had to have some.

Trying to be sensible, I agreed with myself not to take home any flannels unless I knew what I was going to do with them. It didn't take me long to discover that this fabric didn't need a fancy quilt design to show it off. It only needed one simple block to let it shine. FLANNEL NEWBIES was conceived, and the fabrics flew off of the shelf and into my studio. By using simple large shapes, the fear-of-flannel factor is greatly reduced. This quilt is such an easy introduction to working with the scary, stretchy, and misjudged PJ fabric—I conquered my fear and you can, too. Grab a bolt of gorgeous flannel and let's get flying!

Gathering Your Fabrics

The yardages are based on 42" wide fabric.
- Light: black-on-white flannel print: large scale for the blocks and the inner border, 1¾ yd.
- Assorted dark to medium-dark white-on-black flannel prints: varying scales for the blocks, 1½ yd. total
- Medium: white-on-black flannel print, medium scale for the outer border and backing, 6⅛ yd.
- Zinger: black-on-red pick-up sticks print, small scale, ½ yd.
- Batting: 72½" x 72½"
- Binding: ⅞ yd.

Fabric suggestions

Look for a variety of white-on-black flannels with varying scales (figs. 1 and 2, page 18).
- This design is very versatile. You can choose one background, or mix it up by using an assortment of light prints. The background fabric is repeated in

the inner border to allow the quilt center to float. Since the oriental print that I chose actually had a spark of red in it, the choice of a red zinger seemed obvious.

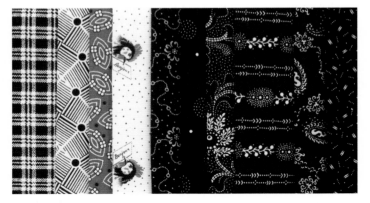

Fig. 1. Keep the darks close in value and vary the scale.

- The black fabrics are an assortment of prints. Choose prints that are close in value but differ in scale to keep the design clean and crisp. The more the merrier for these prints.
- For the outer border, I used a fabric that hadn't yet appeared in the quilt. It is a medium that is really fun. It wasn't dark enough to use in the piecing, so it received top billing as the border and backing.

Fig. 2. For the outer border, go for a print completely different from the other fabrics.

- Because of the crisp clean look I was attempting to achieve, I broke my own rule on using a standout fabric for the binding and used a solid black instead. It adds just the right strength and simplicity to enclose the quilt.

Making Your Newbies Blocks

1. Match up one each of the light background squares with one each of the dark squares, right sides together. Make two diagonal cuts to get four triangles from each pair of squares (fig. 3).

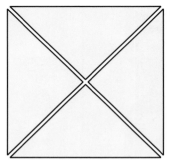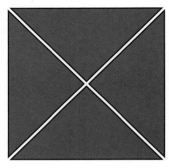

Fig. 3. Cut 4 triangles from each pair of squares.

2. With the dark side down, sew each pair of triangles in the position shown in figure 4. Make sure the dark side is underneath as you sew each pair.

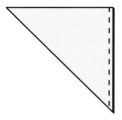

Fig. 4. Sew each pair of triangles with the dark side underneath.

Cutting List
All strips are cut across width of fabric unless otherwise stated. Binding strips are cut on the bias.

Fabric	First Cut (Trim selvages off all strips after first cut.)	Second Cut
Light, 1¾ yd.	4 strips 10"	16 squares 10" x 10" for blocks
	5 strips 3½" for inner border	
Dark, 1½ yd. total	10" strips from each fabric	16 squares 10" x 10" in all for blocks
Medium, 6⅛ yd.	6 strips 10" for outer border	
Zinger, ½ yd.	5 strips 2½" for zinger border	

3. Press the seam allowances open. This is a change from regular piecing where the seam allowances are pressed in one direction. With flannel, pressing the seams open helps reduce the bulk.

4. Mix and match your sewn triangles so that each pair has two different dark print. Place the triangle pairs right sides together and sew the long side (fig. 5). These sets have bias edges, so handle them carefully. Trim the blocks to 9¼" x 9¼".

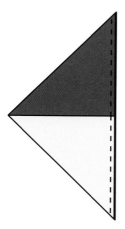

Fig. 5. Sew the long side of the triangles.

5. Join the blocks in rows in an alternating hourglass pattern as shown in the quilt assembly diagram .

Adding the Borders

1. For the inner border, join five 3½" light strips. Cut two 35½" strips and sew one to each side of the quilt. Then cut two 41½" strips and sew them to the top and bottom of the quilt.

2. For the zinger border, join five 2½" strips. Cut two 41½" strips and sew one to each side of the quilt. Then cut two 45½" strips and sew them to the top and bottom of the quilt.

3. For the outer border, join six 10" medium strips. Cut two 45½" strips and sew one to each side of the quilt. Then cut two 64½" strips and sew them to the top and bottom of the quilt.

Finishing Touches

● This is a great quilt to send out to your favorite machine quilter. Because it is flannel, it is bulky and heavy. If you can quilt this on your home machine, you deserve a medal!

● With the quilting, I wanted to contrast the straight lines and sharp points of the piecing, so I used flowing curls to soften the center of the quilt. I used one of my favorite textures, a zigzag line, to add definition to the zinger border. The outer border fabric is so busy that nothing I would have quilted would have shown. It doesn't need to. I just meandered to hold the layers together without disturbing the wonderful pattern of the fabric.

● I have found that binding flannel is not too tricky, but I like to have a little extra binding to work with. Instead of cutting a 2¼" bias binding, which is my usual method, I used a 2½" strip. This gives me just a tad more fabric to ease around the fullness of flannel seam allowances. The binding is still rounded and stuffed but is easier to work with.

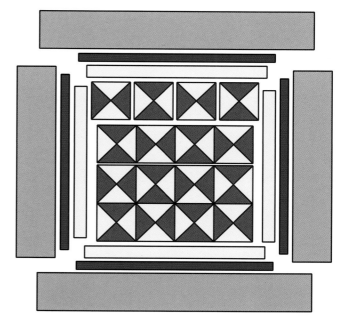

FLANNEL NEWBIES quilt assembly

DIAMONDS?...RUBIES?

48" x 64" Made by the author.

There comes a time in every girl's life when the decisions get tougher and the stakes get higher.

Val had successfully avoided the new guy in 3B for months. She was so focused on advancing her career, she hadn't given his greetings a second thought, much less given him a second glance. If she hadn't dropped her mail in the hall, would she ever have noticed how his hair flopped daringly over his eyebrow, or how his lips curled up into that adorably crooked smile?

As their hands accidentally made contact reaching for her mail, he smiled and asked if she had eaten dinner and would she like to go out and grab a bite. While shaking her head no and meaning to say no, her eyes met his and she started at their crisp blueness.

Before she could swim out of those lovely eyes, Val answered, "Yes, No... I mean no and yes."

"Great! I'll pick you up at 7:00." He was gone before she could think or breathe.

Gathering her mail (and herself), she floated into her apartment wondering why she had never noticed his smile. It wasn't until she locked the door behind her that she realized what she had done. She had made a date with Mr. 3B (who she now realized was absolutely dreamy). What could she have been thinking?

Greeting her and clamoring for attention, even her feline companions, Chloe, Corner, and Clarice, seemed to be chastising her for the momentary lapse. Brushing past them, Val headed for her closet, resigned to her fate. She couldn't back out now. That would be very rude. Grabbing the perfect little black dress from the choices hanging there, she fumbled for her black pumps. She had eighteen minutes left to get ready.

Thankful for her short pixie cut, Val was showered and dressed in a flash. Soon she was powdered, lipsticked, and ready to go. But something was missing. Accessories! Val hurried to her jewelry box. Opening the lid, she was overwhelmed by a new dilemma.

Fearful of making the wrong decision, she asked her kitties, "What should I wear? Diamonds?...Rubies?"

Gathering Your Fabrics

Yardages are based on 42" wide fabric.
- Assorted dark to medium: white-on-black prints, varying scales for the backgrounds. Scraps or yardage to make 48 squares 9" x 9", 3¼ yd. total.
- Assorted red: dark to medium solids, tone-on-tones, and white-on-red prints,

varying scales, for the rubies. These are your zingers. Scraps or yardage at least 6" wide, ¾ yd. total.

- Assorted white: light and medium-light, black-on-white prints, varying scales for the diamonds. Yardage or scraps at least 5½" wide, 1¾ yd. total.
- Backing: 4 yd.
- Batting: 56" x 72"
- Binding: (cut on bias), ⅞ yd.

Fabric suggestions

Clean out your stash for this quilt! You can use all sorts of plaids, prints, uglies, and leftovers, as long as you have contrast (figs. 1, 2, and 3).

- Keep those dark prints dark (occasionally it is fun to add a medium to spice it up a bit) and the light prints light.

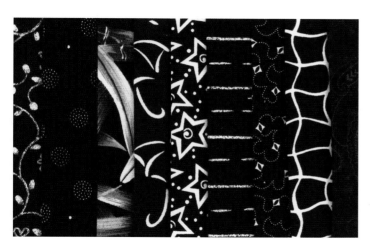

Fig. 1. Go for contrast in your darks.

- Throw in every red you can find! You will be amazed how they blend and add sparkle even when they don't "match."

Fig. 2. The more different reds, the merrier.

- Keep the lights light. Scale and print variations are what make this quilt so much fun. Mix it up and watch your quilt shine.
- I used one fabric for the binding, but you could even scrap up your binding. A scrappy binding won't give the crisp edge that one fabric does, but it could be very interesting.

Fig. 3. Go for variety in scale and prints.

Cutting List All strips are cut across width of fabric unless otherwise stated. Binding strips are cut on the bias.

Fabric	First Cut (Trim selvages off all strips after first cut.)	Second Cut
Blacks, 3¼ yd	12 strips 9"	48 squares 9" x 9"
Reds, ¾ yd	2 strips 3½"	12 squares 3½" x 3½"
	2 strips 6"	12 squares 6" x 6"
Whites, 1¾ yd	3 strips 2½"	36 squares 2½" x 2½"
	4 strips 3½"	36 squares 3½" x 3½"
	5 strips 5"	36 squares 5" x 5"

BLACK & WHITE QUILTS BY DESIGN ● KAY M. CAPPS CROSS   21

Making the Diamonds and Rubies

Raw-edge appliqué adds texture to this quilt. After the first washing, the chenille edges turn the diamond and ruby fabrics into multifaceted gems.

1. Position each 5" light square on point on a black 9" square. Stitch a generous ¼" in from the perimeter of the light square. (fig.4).

Fig. 4. Sew the light squares to the black backgrounds.

2. Layer and sew each light 3½" square over the 5" squares with a ¼" seam. Then repeat this step with each light 2½" square (fig. 5).

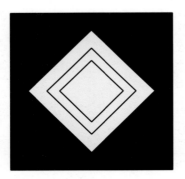

Fig. 5. Sew the remaining diamonds in place.

Note: *If you want to streamline this process, you can layer all three diamonds at one time. Then stitch them in place with the same ¼" seams, starting with the perimeter of the center diamond and working out from there. That's the way I do it.*

3. Cut each diamond into four 4½" quarter-diamond squares (fig. 6).

Fig. 6. Cut four quarter-diamonds.

4. To reduce bulk in the corner, trim away the excess behind the small diamond on the wrong side, leaving ¼" seam allowance (fig. 7).

Fig. 7. Cut away fabric on the wrong side to reduce bulk.

5. To make circles for the rubies, fold each 3½" and 6" red square in four, and then cut an arc from the raw edge of each folded square. Cutting freehand is fine (fig. 8).

Fig. 8. Cut 12 small and 12 large circles from the red squares.

6. Layer and sew each small and large red circle to the remaining 12 black backgrounds the same way you sewed the diamonds.

7. Cut each ruby into four 4½" quarter-ruby squares and trim the excess fabric from behind the small ruby the same way you did with the diamonds.

Making Your Diamond and Ruby Blocks

1. Shuffle your quarter-diamonds into 36 groups with four different quarter-diamonds in each group. Assemble your diamond blocks as shown in figure 9.
2. Shuffle your quarter-rubies into 12 groups with four different quarter-rubies in each group. Assemble your ruby blocks as shown in figure 9.

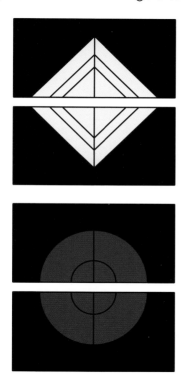

Fig. 9. Diamond and ruby block assembly

3. Sew your blocks into rows according to the quilt assembly diagram.
4. *After* you quilt and bind your quilt, toss it in the washing machine and put it through a gentle cycle. Then toss it in the dryer to soften those raw edges.

Note: *Do not leave this quilt in the dryer unattended. Check your lint trap frequently to prevent your dryer from overheating.*

Finishing Touches

- I have quilted this design in many ways. The original of this quilt has the names for all of the registered diamond cuts quilted on it. That took some research!
- I have also emphasized the shapes of the stones by quilting circles in the rubies and squares in the diamonds. You could also meander in all of the background sections and do a design in the stones.
- If you like to tie quilts, this design has that old-fashioned flavor that would lend itself to tying with some coordinating perle cotton or high quality yarn.
- You can experiment with batting versus no batting with this quilt. The built-in weight from layering would be substantial enough for a summer quilt with flannel backing.
- However you choose to connect the layers, don't forget to bind your quilt with a binding that stands out and sparkles.
- Don't forget to date and sign your quilt.

Now you are ready to make that important decision, "What should I wear? Diamonds?...Rubies?"

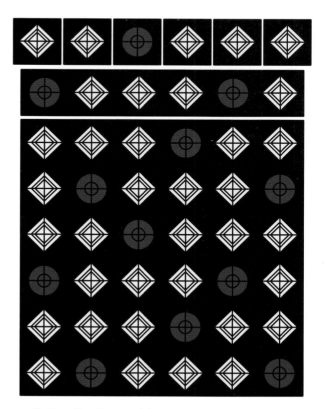

DIAMONDS?...RUBIES? quilt assembly

FOOLS TRAVEL IN 4-PACKS

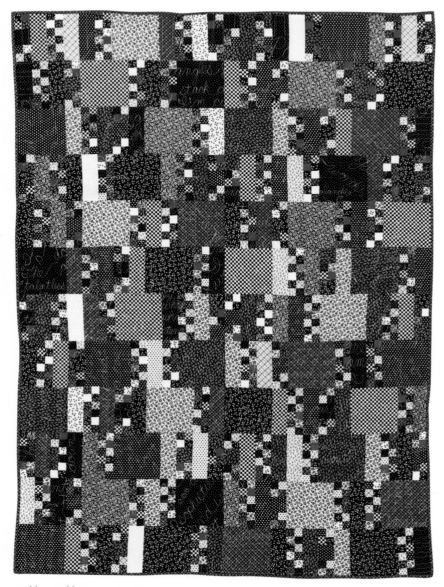

52½" x 72½" Made by the author.

My life greatly improved at 40. It was around that time that I met three remarkable women who have become the "fools" in my 4-pack. Quilting is the common thread that brought us together. Friendship and mutual respect is the glue that keeps us together. The four of us come from very different backgrounds and eras. We have different beliefs and lifestyles, but we are able to come together to share life and joy and fun. We take each other as we are and celebrate our differences and similarities. We have found such a comfortable rapport with one another, I can't imagine my life without them.

We're in almost daily contact through e-mails laced with humor and wisdom. We make time in our busy lives to see each other whenever we can. And every year we go on a quilting retreat together. We tend to get quite silly on these retreats. We stay up too late and laugh just enough. We play, talk, quilt, recharge our creative batteries, and mostly, we're not afraid to be a little foolish together.

It was on one of our retreats that we found some little stuffed animals in a gift shop. Foolish as it sounds, when we saw these delicious little critters, we knew they needed us. We each adopted one as our personal mascot. At the end of the retreat, they traveled home with us in a 4-pack juice container, where, like us, they fit together perfectly.

This quilt is my tribute to the four of us and our friendship. How fortunate I am in this life to have found a 4-pack of friends that lift me up, challenge me, and allow me to be a caring, loving friend in return. Like our little mascots, we're content to know that fools travel in 4-packs.

Gathering Your Fabrics

Yardages are based on 42" wide fabric.
- Dark: assorted dark to medium dark, white-on-black prints, small to medium scale. Scraps or yardage, 3 yd. total.
- Medium: assorted medium-light and medium-dark, white-on-black and black-on-white prints, varying scales. Scraps or yardage, 2¼ yd. total.
- Light: assorted light to medium-light, black-on-white prints, varying scales. Scraps or yardage: 1¼ yd. total.
- Zinger: red tone-on-tone print, ¼ yd.
- Backing: 4½ yd.
- Batting: 60½" x 80½"
- Binding (cut on bias): ¾ yd.

Fabric suggestions

In order to get the playful movement in this quilt, you will need to be attentive to value (figs. 1–3).

- Keep your darks very dark and your lights very light. Their values should be clear, with no confusion with mediums.

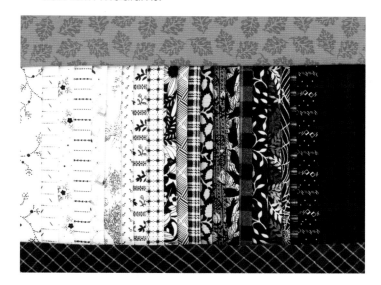

Fig. 1. Select fabrics that are clearly dark. Avoid medium-darks.

- Use a variety of prints and scales for the lights. Go for some really light pieces. The light fabrics in this quilt provide the resting for the eye. So don't use a light that could be a medium. That would muddy the waters and reduce the clarity of the design.
- The medium selections have the most fluidity in the quilt. The bulk of your medium fabrics should be clearly medium. However, a few ambiguous pieces among the mediums will add movement and surprises in the piecing.

Fig. 2. Keep the values of the darks and lights clearly separate.

- Figure 3 is an example of a few vague value choices whose fluctuation will add wonderful motion to the quilt.

Fig. 3. The mediums in this collection vacillate between dark and medium.

Cutting List
All strips are cut across width of fabric unless otherwise stated. Binding strips are cut on the bias.

Fabric	First Cut (Trim selvages off all strips after first cut.)	Second Cut
Dark, 3 yd.	20 strips 1½"	39 strips 1½" x 21" for four-patch units
	11 strips 2½"	43 rectangles 2½" x 6½"
		40 squares 2½" x 2½"
	4 strips 6½"	21 squares 6½" x 6½"
Medium, 2¼ yd.	10 strips 1½"	19 strips 1½" x 21" for four-patch units
	6 strips 2½"	37 rectangles 2½" x 6½"
	4 strips 6½"	19 squares 6½" x 6½"
Light, 1¼ yd.	10 strips 2½"	20 strips 2½" x 21" for four-patch units
	3 strips 2½"	16 rectangles 2½" x 6½"
Zinger, ¼ yd.	3 strips 1½"	6 strips 1½" x 21" for four-patch units

- I pieced my back with remainders of the light fabrics and a few of the lighter mediums. This can be a great way to use the tail ends of the fabrics and add excitement to the back of your quilt. You spend a lot of time and money on the top—it deserves an attractive and quality back.

- The quality of your fabric selections should carry over to the binding as well. Don't stop short of a polished project by using something ineffective for the binding. I think of binding as a quilt's punctuation. I punctuate my quilts with exclamation points.

Making Four-Patch Units

1. Match pairs of 1½" x 21" strips in the combinations shown in figure 4, and sew the pairs into strip-sets. It would seem more efficient to start with 42" strips, but cutting them in half first gives you a chance to create more variety in the strip-sets.

Make 18 black/medium strip-sets.

Make 18 white/black strip-sets.

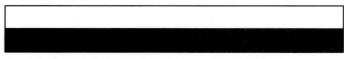

Make 2 white/zinger strip-sets.

Make 3 black/zinger strip-sets.

Make 1 medium/zinger strip-set.

Fig. 4. Sew strip-sets.

2. Match pairs of strip-sets right-sides together according to the table in figure 5. Make sure you keep the strips positioned top and bottom exactly as shown. Cut each pair of strip-sets into 1½" segments, maintaining the positions of the segments exactly as shown.

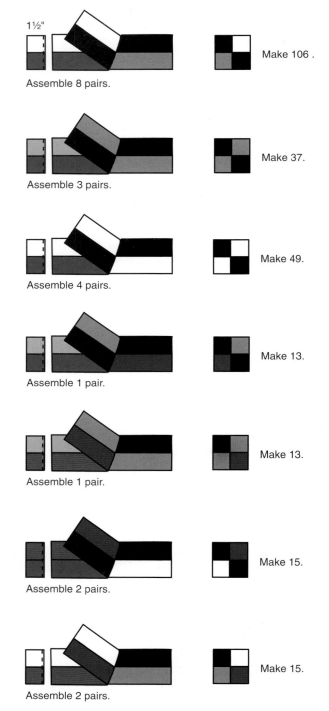

Fig. 5. Place strip-sets right-sides together. Cut 1½" segment pairs.

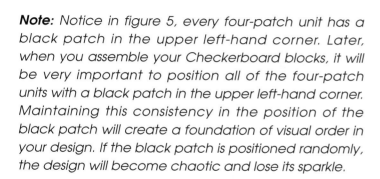

Note: *Notice in figure 5, every four-patch unit has a black patch in the upper left-hand corner. Later, when you assemble your Checkerboard blocks, it will be very important to position all of the four-patch units with a black patch in the upper left-hand corner. Maintaining this consistency in the position of the black patch will create a foundation of visual order in your design. If the black patch is positioned randomly, the design will become chaotic and lose its sparkle.*

3. Keep the segment pairs with the same side up as shown in figure 5 and sew them together into four-patch units with the stitching on the right (fig. 6). Press the units open.

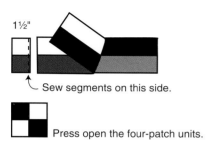

1½"

└ Sew segments on this side.

Press open the four-patch units.

Fig. 6. Stitch on the right.

Assembling Your Blocks and Rows

There are three kinds of blocks to make with your four-patch units (fig. 7). Checkerboards have 3 four-patch units. The Bookend blocks have 1 solid square between 2 four-patch units, and the Sandwich blocks have 1 four-patch unit sandwiched between 2 solid squares.

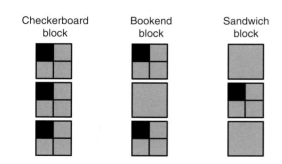

Checkerboard block	Bookend block	Sandwich block

Fig 7. Three kinds of Four-Patch blocks.

1. As shown in the first row of the quilt assembly diagram on page 28, assemble 62 Checkerboard blocks, 28 Bookend blocks, and 6 Sandwich blocks. Use these blocks along with rectangles and large squares to assemble the first row.
2. Make the blocks for the next row and follow the quilt diagram to assemble the second row.
3. Repeat step 2 until all of the rows are assembled. As you complete the rows you can sew them together and watch your quilt grow, or you can wait and sew them all together at the end.

Finishing Touches

- Since this quilt is a tribute to us, I used our own words to quilt the top. Our 4-pack is prolific not only in quiltmaking, but also in spewing forth pearls of wisdom. The quilting is taken directly from our e-mail conversations.
- Crosshatching would work beautifully on this quilt, as would straight line quilting.
- Fanciful circles or swirls would also be fun on this highly structured quilt top. It often works well to contrast the straight lines of a quilt with fluid circular shapes or lines. Contrast is important in color and shape.
- The binding is an important element of the design. The binding frames and defines the quilt top. A weak binding weakens the whole effect of the quilt. Be brave and make a bold choice in binding fabric. You will be glad that you did.
- Don't neglect to sign or label your quilt. Take pride in your accomplishment. Your children's grandchildren will thank you. They won't have to try to figure out who made the quilt, and why. You will have left them a piece of their family history, complete with the date and the quiltmaker's name.

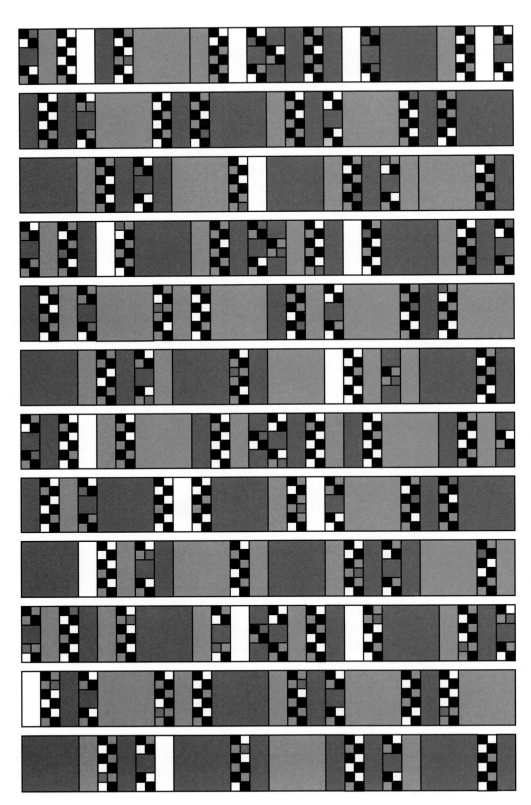

Fig. 8. FOOLS TRAVEL IN 4-PACKS quilt assembly

WINTER PINES

38½" x 46½" Made by the author.

I grew up spending my summers in our family's cabin by the lake. It is no surprise that I find the trees of Wisconsin so inspiring.

Now that I'm grown, we often take our children to the cabin to spend the weekend. It is an easy two-and-a-half hour drive through many beautiful scenes to enjoy. My favorites are the stately rows of pine trees. Some of the rows are tall and separated. Some are full and lush. One particular stand of pines always elicits a response from me as we drive by. After listening to me ooh and ah for years, my husband finally said, "Why don't you put it in a quilt?" Gosh, what an idea! No wonder I married him.

The result of his suggestion was my first foray into using only black and white to capture what I see in my mind's eye. I wanted to celebrate the beauty and dignity of the pines without the distraction of color. Of course I had to add just a dash of color since no stand of pines is complete without that flash of a cardinal or other some other feathered visitor.

As I made my first WINTER PINES, I knew I had found something that really satisfied my creative soul. I could see my interpretation of the pines in my head and actually reproduce it with fabric. Life is good.

Gathering Your Fabrics

Yardages are based on fabrics 42" wide.

- Dark backgrounds and trees: assorted dark and medium-dark white-on-black prints, varying scales. Yardage or scraps, 1⅓ yd. total.
- Light backgrounds and trees: assorted light and medium black-on-white prints, varying scales. Yardage or scraps, 1⅓ yd. total.
- Zinger for cornerstones: red tone-on-tone print, ⅛ yd.
- Lattice: medium, black-on-gray print, medium scale, ⅜ yd.
- Inner border: medium-dark, white paisley on black print, large scale, ¼ yd.
- Outer border: dark, white dots on black print, small scale, ¾ yd.
- Backing: 3 yd.
- Batting: 46" x 54"
- Binding: ⅝ yd.
- Foundation fabric 12" wide: 5 yd.

Fabric suggestions

Choose fabrics that are similar in value, but have scale variations for the dark and light fabrics (figs. 1–4, page 30).

- A few wayward pieces that could be either light or dark can add to the fun. Their value will depend on what you place them next to.

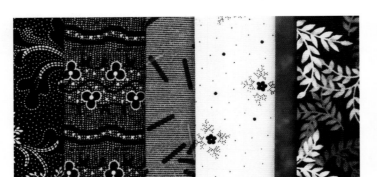

Fig. 1. The occasional misfit in a color group adds some fun.

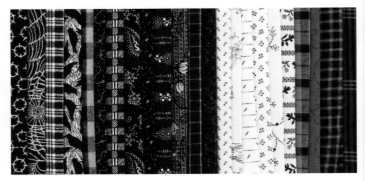

Fig. 3. Use prints with lines that will run into each other when they're set side-by-side.

- You could use one fabric for all of the dark backgrounds and trees and one fabric for all of the light backgrounds and trees.
- The lattice fabric is wonderful when done in a stripe or vertical pattern. It should be a medium, but blend well with the inner border.

Fig. 2. A stripe or vertical print makes the lattice stand out.

- The inner border and outer border should be at least one step away from each other in value. The quilt will be framed by the deepening values of the borders.
- It is fun to trick the eye by having prints in neighboring fabrics bleed into one another and appear to be one fabric, until you take a closer look.

- The zinger cornerstone fabric should pop right out. Make it intense and bright.
- You can never go wrong with a stripe on the bias for the binding. Checks or a plaid are also great choices.

Fig. 4. A bright and vibrant zinger doesn't have to be red to pop out.

Making Winter Pine Blocks

1. With a transfer pen, trace one copy of each tree pattern onto seven foundation squares. Add ¼" seam allowances around each block. Press to transfer these onto seven additional foundation squares. Each copy will give you the reverse image of the first tracing. You now have 14 foundations.

Cutting List All strips are cut across width of fabric unless otherwise stated. Binding strips are cut on the bias.

Fabric	First Cut (Trim selvages off all strips after first cut.)	Second Cut
Dark backgrounds and trees, 1⅓ yd.	an assortment of 3", 4", and 5" strips	
Light backgrounds and trees, 1⅓ yd.	an assortment of 3", 4", and 5" strips	
Lattice, ⅜ yd.	10 strips 1"	49 strips 1" x 8"
Zinger, ⅛ yd.	1 strip 1"	30 squares 1" x 1"
Inner border, ¼ yd.	4 strips 1½"	
Outer border, ¾ yd.	5 strips 2½"	
Foundation fabric, 5 yd.	20 squares 8½" x 8½"	

2. Pick your three favorite trees and press to transfer these to six additional foundation squares. You now have a total of 20 foundations.

3. Piece 10 foundations with dark backgrounds and light trees. Then piece 10 foundations with light backgrounds and dark trees.

4. Trim your completed blocks to 8" squares.

Assembling Your Rows

1. Alternating dark and light backgrounds, assemble five rows, beginning and ending with a lattice strip, as shown in the quilt assembly diagram.

2. Sew six horizontal lattice strips, beginning and ending with a zinger cornerstone.

3. Join the rows and horizontal lattice strips as shown in the quilt assembly diagram.

Adding the Borders

1. For the inner border, join four 1½" medium strips. Cut two 41" strips and sew one to each side of the quilt. Then cut two 35" strips and sew them to the top and bottom of the quilt.

2. For the outer border, join five 2½" dark strips. Cut two 43" strips and sew one to each side of the quilt. Then cut two 39" strips and sew them to the top and bottom of the quilt.

Finishing Touches

- WINTER PINES truly offers so many options for quilting. It is small enough to quilt on your home machine and big enough to send off to your favorite longarm quilter.

- The density of the quilting needs to be fairly equal on all sections of the quilt to keep it flatter.

- I like to quilt the background of the trees heavily to allow the trees to jump out from the quilt. I have used zigzags, stippling, and echo stitching—all sorts of things.

- I wait to quilt the trees until the very end. I like to do the least amount possible, which gives the trees more texture and lift.

- I usually quilt the borders in straight lines to frame the quilt. I don't want to detract from the trees.

- The most important thing to remember is that the quilting should please you. Make it a piece that brings you joy. If it pleases your eye, it is just right.

- Don't forget the snazzy binding! Take ownership and pride in your work by signing it or adding a personalized label. You worked hard, so celebrate your talents!

Hang up your WINTER PINES and enjoy the crisp, icy winter all year 'round!

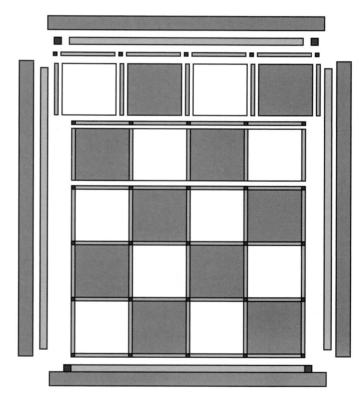

WINTER PINES quilt assembly

Winter Pines Tree A

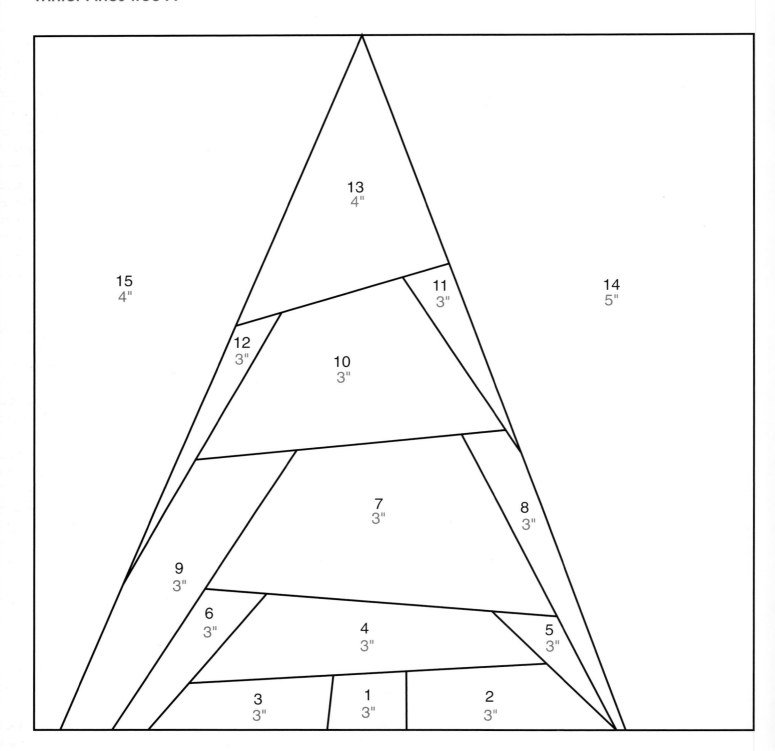

Add ¼" seam allowance around the outside of the block.

Winter Pines Tree B

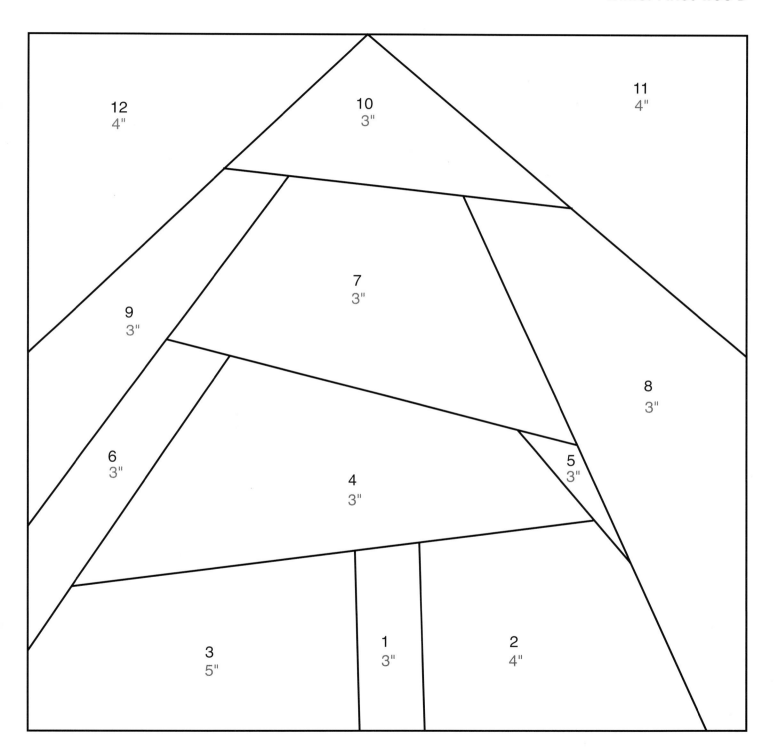

Add ¼" seam allowance around the outside of the block.

Winter Pines Tree C

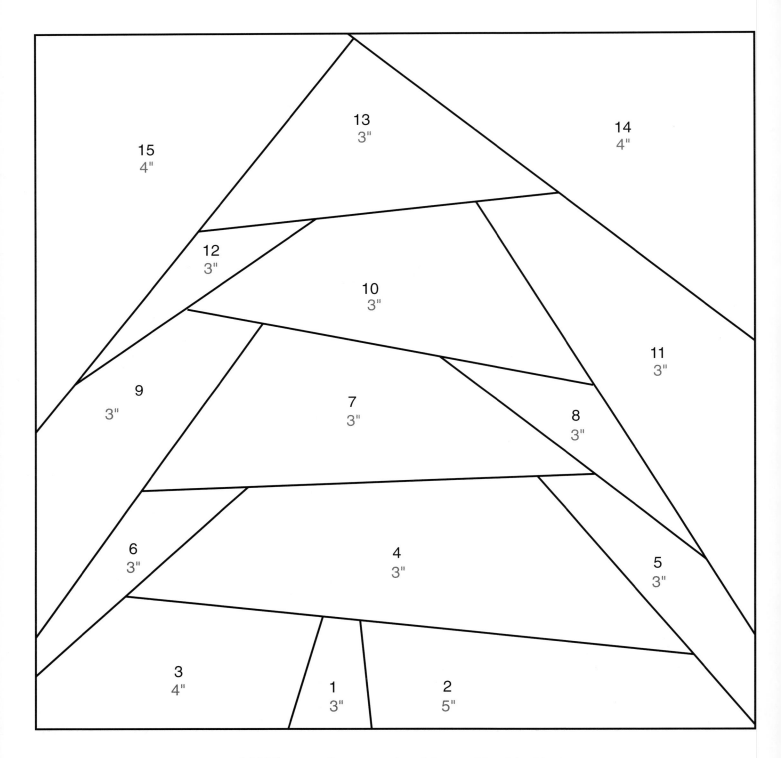

Add ¼" seam allowance around the outside of the block.

Winter Pines Tree D

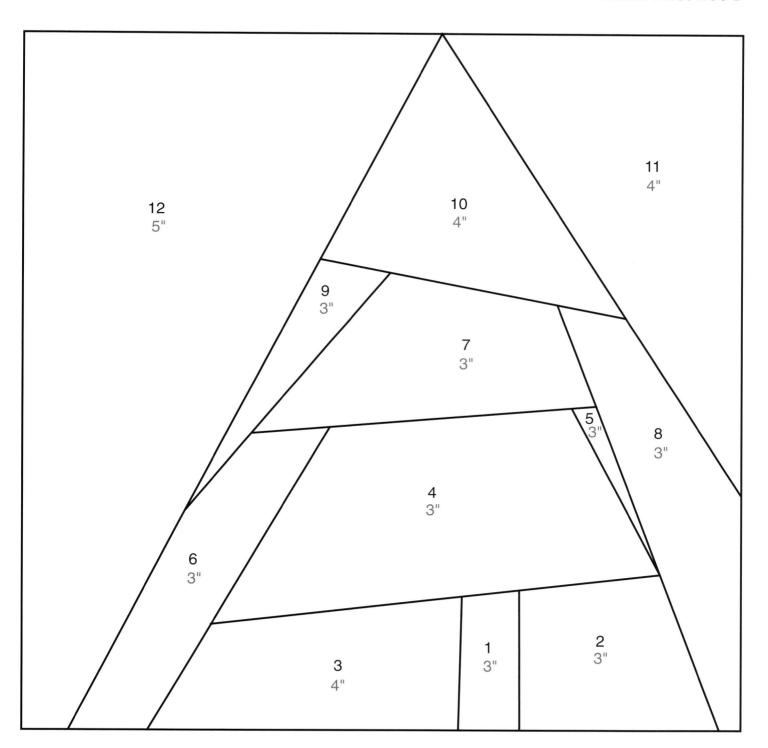

Add ¼" seam allowance around the outside of the block.

Winter Pines Tree E

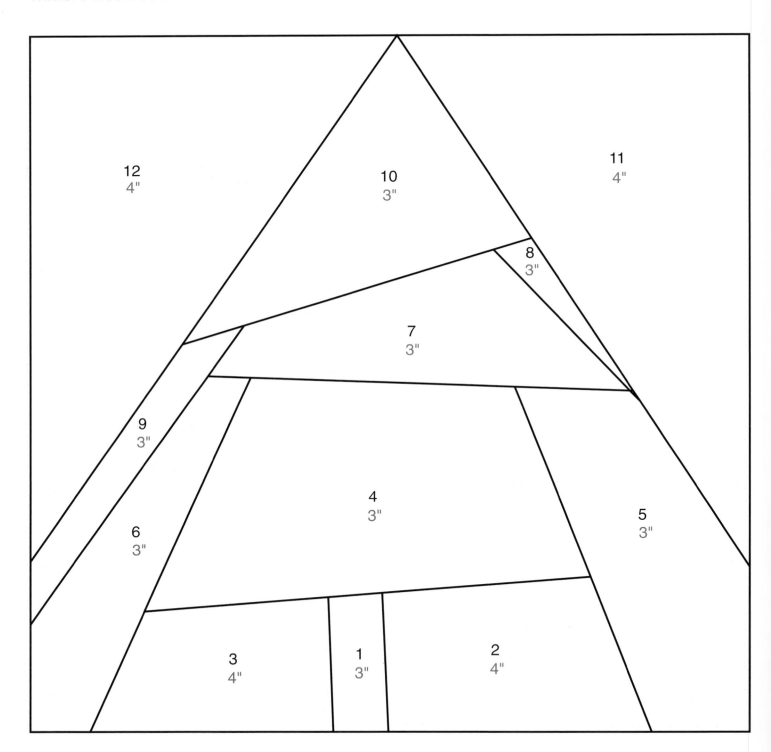

12
4"

10
3"

11
4"

8
3"

7
3"

9
3"

4
3"

6
3"

5
3"

3
4"

1
3"

2
4"

Add ¼" seam allowance around the outside of the block.

Winter Pines Tree F

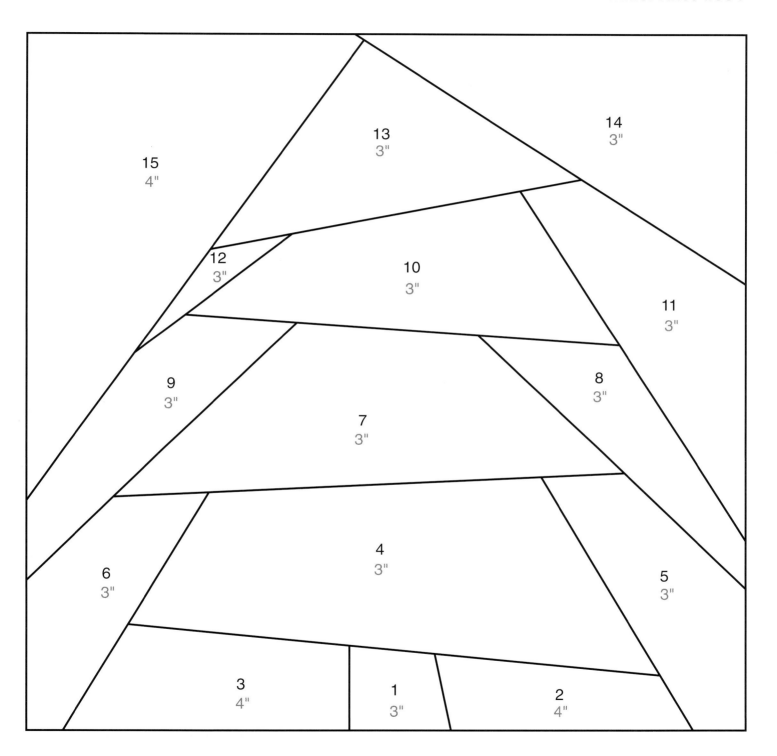

Add ¼" seam allowance around the outside of the block.

Winter Pines Tree G

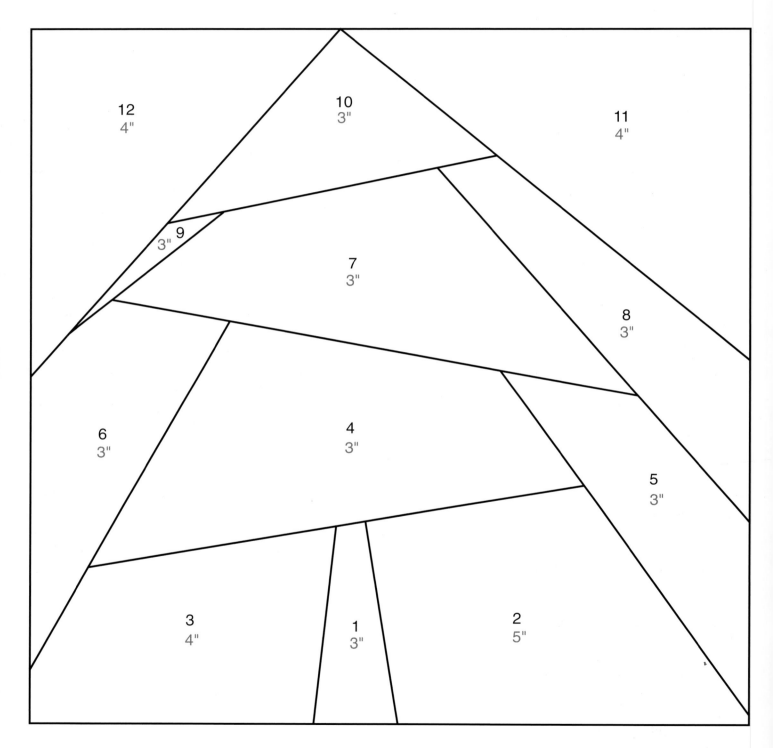

12
4"

10
3"

11
4"

9
3"

7
3"

8
3"

6
3"

4
3"

5
3"

3
4"

1
3"

2
5"

Add ¼" seam allowance around the outside of the block.

64" x 64" Made by the author.

I absolutely love this quilt. It embodies so much of what I try to teach and how I try to live. It echoes how I like to spend my day.

I know my day will be framed within the confines of a twenty-four hour "block." but the opportunities and experiences available within those hours are unpredictable and exciting.

I admire quilters who can work methodically and meticulously to create incredible works of art. Their quilts have tidy, well trimmed backs hidden behind crisp corners and arrow-straight seams. Their stashes are neatly folded in logical arrays of color while work surfaces are clear and at the ready. Order and logic support their creativity and productivity. How I wish I could assimilate some of those wonderful habits.

But, alas, I function in artistic chaos. I compose quilts from scraps scattered on numerous horizontal surfaces. I scribble ideas on bank deposit slips and file them in various corners of the studio. I abandon current projects for the fresh idea hatched in last night's dream.

I could berate myself for the lack of order and organization in

my day. Or, I could delight in the surprises and joys that accompany a life in a household with four children. With all of the choices presented to me, I opt for a life of muddled, untidy, and unpredictable bliss.

This quilt is a happy mix of order and serendipity, randomness and rules. First, I am inviting you to make a play date with your stash. Choose your fabrics with abandon for this quilt, but follow the rules in the fabric suggestions. Then, as you build the blocks, enjoy grabbing any random strip without worrying if it is the right one for that block. (Trust me, it will be right.) But carefully follow the Rules of the Game given in the instructions. The randomness will make your quilt dance; the rules will control the chaos. The results will be wonderful.

I hope you will embrace whatever choice suits you. Honor whatever type of quilter you are. And most importantly, leave time to play. For this quilt, enjoy being both meticulous and slaphappy.

Gathering Your Fabrics

- Light to medium-light: assorted white-on-white, multicolor-on-white, and black-on-white prints, small and medium scales. Yardage and scraps, 4 yd. total.
- Dark to medium-dark: assorted black-on-black, multicolor-on-black, and white-on-black prints, small and medium scales. Scraps and yardage, 4 yd. total.
- Zinger: assorted red prints and solids. Any odd-shaped scraps and yardage, 1¾ yd. total.
- Muslin for foundation squares: 4⅜ yd.
- Backing: 4 yd.
- Binding: ¾ yd.
- Batting: none

Fabric suggestions

Pull out all of the stops with this quilt. Gather up all those black prints that you have had for years and toss them in with some new prints (figs. 1–3).

- Black-and-white prints will mix up nicely with a few prints that have splashes of the red zinger. Use those prints sparingly to preserve the strong graphic quality of the quilt.
- Use mostly dark prints, but do throw in a few medium dark prints.

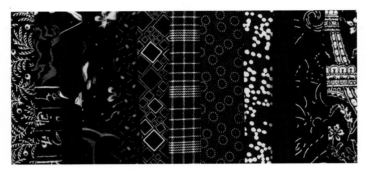

Fig. 1. Keep the darks dark and go for variety in the prints.

- I dare you to throw in an old black calico!
- Use up that black solid from a Halloween costume from 20 years ago.
- Vary the scale with the red zinger prints. Vary the value slightly, but keep the color intense to allow the diamonds to pop out of the quilt.

Fig. 2. Throw in some clashing reds with your zingers.

- For the zingers, mix true red, red-orange, red-violet, and any other kind of red you can find. It is amazing how fabrics that appear to clash give a quilt life and spark in this quilt.
- Don't forget to mix plaids, stripes, checks, florals, and anything else you stumble on.

Fig. 3. Use whites with as many different personalities as you can find.

- Variety is also the key for the white prints. Don't limit yourself to white-on-white or white with black. Toss in some off-white, ecru, and maybe even some unbleached muslin.
- A few of your white prints could have touches of red. Keep the prints toward the light end of the value spectrum.
- Since you are staying away from medium-value prints with the black fabrics, you can lob a very few medium-value white prints into the mix for a surprise. They will add texture and keep the eyes moving across the quilt surface.

Rules of the Game

The piecing in this quilt appears to be completely random. It is true that you will pick fabric strips randomly, and the widths of the strips within each block vary. But there is an underlying order that makes this quilt work. Study the individual blocks in the SLAPHAPPY quilt

Cutting List	All strips are cut across width of fabric unless otherwise stated. Binding strips are cut on the bias.
Fabric	**Strip (Trim selvages off all strips after first cut.)**
Darks and whites, 8 yd	From yardage, cut strips a variety of widths from 1" to 2½"
Zinger, 1¾ yd	From yardage, cut 52 squares 3½" x 3½" and
	12 rectangles 2½" x 4½". Use odd-shaped scraps as is.
Muslin, 4⅜ yd	64 squares 9" x 9"

pictured on page 39. Compare them to the block in figure 4 and notice the following consistencies:

six light and five dark strips

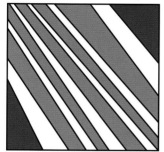

Fig. 4. Make 64 blocks .

- Every block has 2 zingers and exactly 11 strips—6 white and 5 dark. The zingers are in opposite corners. The strips next to the zingers are always white.
- The strips in most blocks are set roughly on the diagonal. In a few blocks, the angle is much steeper. This exception to the angle rule happens when you start with a narrow zinger rectangle. As long as you limit the number of these steep-angled blocks, they add movement to the quilt and help enhance the impression of randomness.
- The widths of the strips within each block vary. But whether they are narrow or wide, most strips are the same width all the way across the block. In some blocks, a strip is wider on one side than on the other. These maverick strips add movement to the quilt, but too many of them would create chaos rather than interest.
- Have confidence in your original fabric selections and let randomness rule as you reach for each strip to add to a block. In other words, no peeking.

Piecing Your Blocks

1. As you cut your strips, sort the darks, lights, and zingers into three paper grocery bags. This keeps the strips from carpeting your sewing room as you work and makes it harder to see which one you are grabbing. When the grocery bags are full, start sewing.
2. Pick up one zinger square at random and place it right-side up on one corner of the foundation square. Make sure the zinger edges overlap the foundation edges (fig. 5).

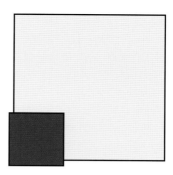

Fig. 5. Place the zinger right-side up.

3. Pull one strip at random from the whites and place it diagonally on the zinger, right-sides together. Make sure the ends of the of the white strip overlap the edges of the foundation by at least 2½". For wider strips, increase the overlap. Sew the zinger and the white strip to the foundation with a ¼" seam, and trim the excess zinger fabric from the seam allowance (fig. 6).

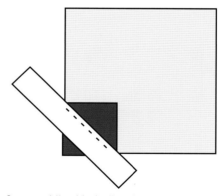

Fig. 6. Sew a white strip to the zinger, right-sides together.

4. Flip over the strip so it is right-side up and finger press. Trim the excess from both ends of the white strip (fig. 7).

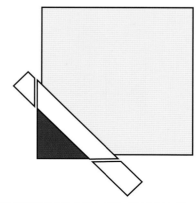

Fig. 7. Flip and finger press the strip, then trim the excess.

5. Repeat steps 3 and 4, alternating black strips with white strips and varying their widths. Keep an eye on how many strips you are using. When you get halfway across the foundation, you should have about six strips sewn on. If you have too many or too few, adjust the widths of the remaining strips so you end with a white strip and have 11 strips in all with some room left to add the second zinger.

6. If you start to run out of white or dark strips, go back to the cutting table and refill your grocery bags. Use your zinger rectangles to make blocks with the strips set on steeper angles.

Assembling Your Quilt

1. With the foundation side up, trim your blocks to squares 8½".

2. Assemble the blocks in rows, according to the quilt assembly diagram. Then sew the rows together.

Finishing Touches

- Because the foundation piecing adds so much weight to the quilt, I did not use batting. I simply backed the quilt with flannel.
- I quilted simple freehand squares inside each block. I wanted to avoid quilting through any of the very thick seams.
- You could tie this for an old-fashioned look.
- It would be logical to bind this visually active quilt with a solid, secure black. That would punctuate and define the quilt beautifully. On the other hand, I really enjoy the way a bias gingham binding outlines the quilt with ambiguity. When I let the design undulate off the edge of the quilt, I am recognizing and saluting endless possibilities.
- Add a label to honor your work.

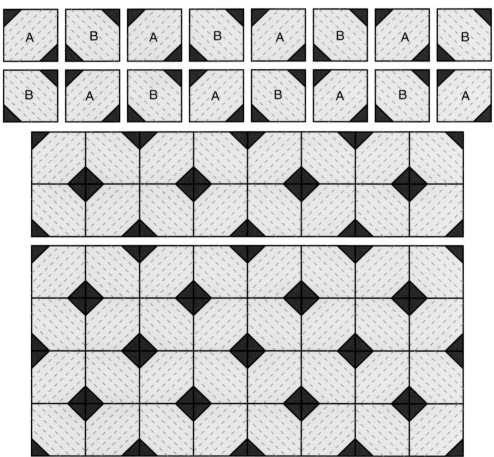

SLAPHAPPY quilt assembly

47½" x 25½" Made by the author.

I made this quilt long before the film *March of the Penguins* documented the patient endurance and determination required of the Emperor penguins to raise their young in the harsh Arctic winter. The baby penguins in this quilt represent my four children.

In the quilt, the babies are marching in a straight line, but rarely have my babies been in such a neat formation in my life. They have kept me busy learning four different ways to communicate, comfort, love, support and discipline, and to view the world through their eyes. Often there is one facing in the opposite direction from the rest of us. They are my joy and the hardest work I've ever done.

Gone are the days when two kiddoes trailed behind me while I had one baby in the carrier and one on my hip. These are the days when I'm running to games and plays and school to watch them grow and play. The march is reversed as they keep me hopping to see all they've learned and accomplished and enjoyed. With the cold winds in the world pushing our children in every direction, you could say that raising our young requires its own kind of endurance and determination. I'm so thankful that, when the day is done, my children seek the warmth of our home and that it is me they tell, "Mama, it's cold outside!"

Gathering Your Fabrics

You will need four fabrics for this quilt. The yardages are based on 42" wide fabric.

- Background: light, black-on-white shirting print, small scale, 1½ yd.

- Belly and neck: medium-light, mottled pink, ¼ yd.
- Beak: medium, red-orange solid. Scraps or ⅛ yd.
- Underwing and binding: medium, black-and-white check, small scale, ⅞ yd.
- Body and border: black solid, 1 yd.
- Ribbon trim: pink 1¼" ribbon trim, 4¼ yd.
- Foundation fabric (12" wide): 3 yd.
- Backing: 1⅝ yd.
- Batting: 55" x 33"

Fabric suggestions

The right fabrics will make your tuxedoed friends stand out in the Arctic winter (figs. 1and 2).

- Use an icy cold background. I used one that had a figure in it that could be taken for snowflakes.
- I really like the pink belly. If you decide to use a different pale color or another white, make sure there is enough contrast between the background and the belly.
- Use a very dark black for the birds and border. You could even use different fabrics for the birds and border. If you do, use the darkest black for the border. That will give you the needed contrast with the ribbon trim.
- I used vintage hand-beaded trim from a sari in India. Dig through your stash—you can use anything.
- Have fun with the underwing check. I used a simple gingham check to set off the solid wing. Go for a change in value and scale.

Fig. 1. The darker the darks, the better the contrast.

Fig. 2. Play with value and scale.

Cutting List
All strips are cut across width of fabric unless otherwise stated . Binding strips are cut on the bias.

Fabric	Strips
Background, 1½ yd.	three 3"
	two 4"
	three 5"
	one 6"
	one 7½"
Belly and neck, ¼ yd.	one 3½"
	one 2"
Beak, ⅛ yd.	one 1"
Underwing and binding, ⅞ yd.	one 1½"
Body and border, 1 yd.	three 3" for body
	four 5½" for border
Foundation fabric, 3 yd.	4 pieces 4½" x 7½" for baby snouts and tails
	4 pieces 8½" x 10" for baby bodies
	2 pieces 7" x 11⅝" for the mama snout and tail
	1 piece 12" x 20" for the mama body

- Don't forget to spend some time considering your binding. Checks always add interest and definition.

Making Your Penguins

1. With a transfer pen, trace one copy of the baby penguin tail and the snout sections onto one 4½" x 7½" foundation piece, leaving at least ¾" between the two sections. Trace one copy of the body onto one 8½" x 10" foundation piece. You can mark the numbers for the penguin pieces. The numbers may show through the light background fabrics, so try to do without those numbers on the foundations.

2. Add a ¼" seam allowance all around each pattern section. This will be the foundation for the baby penguin on the right of the quilt. Remember, in foundation piecing, your final block will be the mirror image of the pattern on the foundation piece.

3. Press to transfer these tracings onto the remaining 4½" x 7½" and 8½" x 10" foundation pieces. You now have the foundations for three babies facing to the left.

4. Enlarge the pattern 175%. Trace one of each section and add a ¼" seam allowance around each pattern section.

5. For the babies, piece each section. The strip widths to use for the pieces are shown on the pattern. Press each section well and trim it along the cutting lines.

6. Flip the traced foundation pieces over and retrace the stitching lines on the other side of the foundation. This is the side you will sew on. This will make the finished mama penguin face to the left.

7. Assemble each penguin according to the diagram in figure 3.

8. From the 7½" background strip, cut one strip 2½" x 7½" and one strip 4½" x 7½". Sew these to the top and bottom of one baby penguin according to the quilt assembly diagram on page 46. Cut three strips 6½" x 7½" and sew them to the tops of the remaining three penguins. Press the seam allowances toward the rectangles.

9. Trim 2" off the left side of the mama block and ¾" off the right side so the mama block measures 9½" x 15½". Sew all four penguins together according to the quilt assembly diagram.

Adding the Borders

1. For the inner border, join three 5½" background strips. Cut two 15½" strips and sew one to each side of the quilt. Then cut two 47½" strips and sew them to the top and bottom of the quilt.

2. Pin and hand sew the ribbon trim on top of the border 1" from the edges of the penguin blocks. Depending on the type of ribbon you use, you can miter the corners or make do.

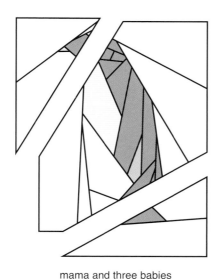
mama and three babies

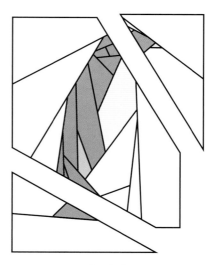
last baby

Fig. 3. Penguin assembly diagram

Finishing Touches

- Because of the simplicity of the design and the few fabrics, I played with creating texture with the machine quilting.
- I enjoy using words that enhance the quilt. I used the title and parallel straight lines to quilt the border outside the ribbon. Inside the ribbon I used a zigzag line that adds dimension.
- I completely avoided quilting the ribbon. It poufs out beautifully that way.

- Vertical quilting lines in the background emphasize the rigid posture of the marching penguins. An occasional snowflake also found its way into the background quilting.
- Mama and her babies need very simple quilting. I added some texture to their bellies and outline stitched the underwing checks. I also did some parallel lines on the wing and back. A little goes a long way to add dimension.

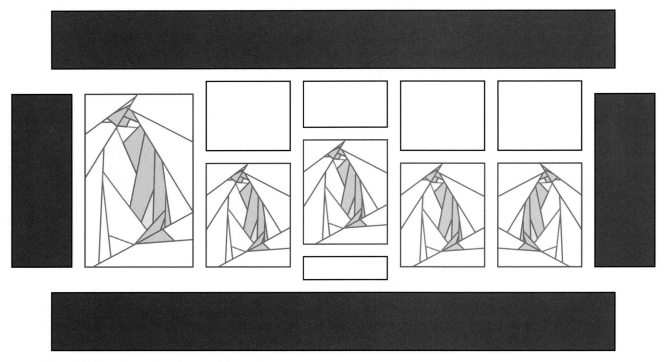

MAMA, IT'S COLD OUTSIDE! quilt assembly

Enlarge 175% for Mama Pattern

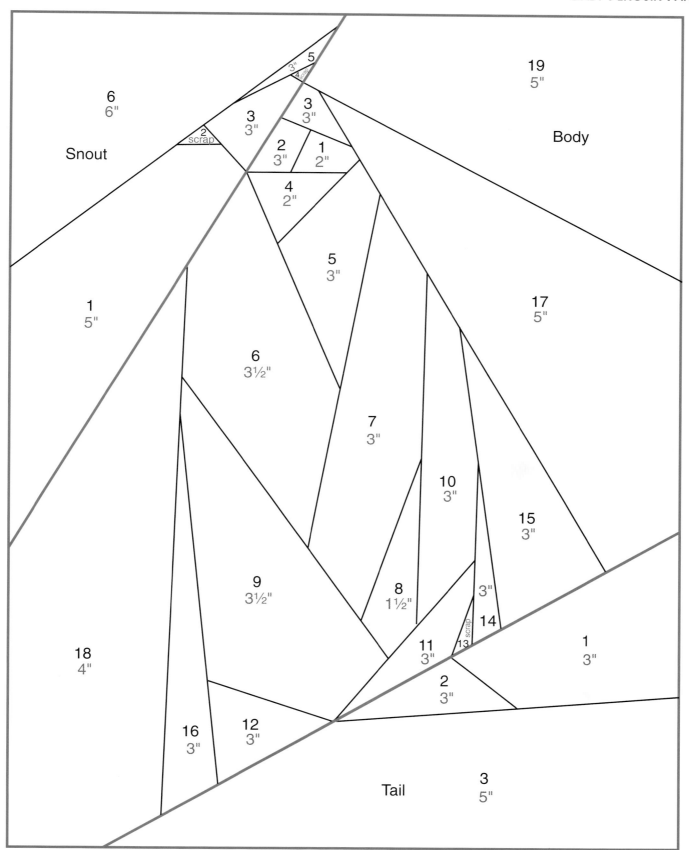

Sections are outlined in red.

Add ¼" seam allowance around each traced section.

Cave Ungulum

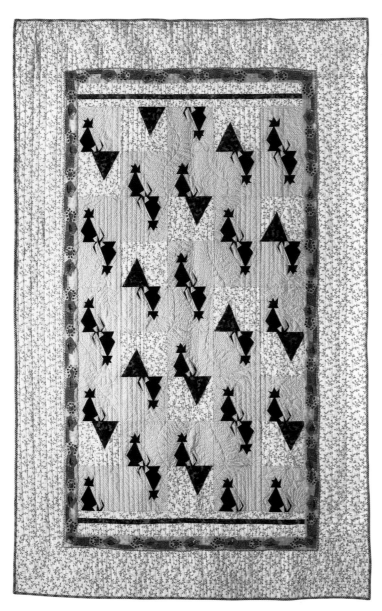

57" x 96" Made by the author.

Long ago, there was this human claw, (a grandfather's seemingly menacing hand) that I was sure was tormenting my first born. The hand was accompanied by the words "Beware the claw!" (Cave ungulum). Being a naturally overprotective and hovering mama, I took offense at this game. While I thought my son must be apprehensive, it quickly became clear to me that he enjoyed this game with his grandpa.

The lesson from that memory is at the core of this quilt. What appeared to be menacing and damaging was in fact my father-in-law's loving hand. I had to strip away my own apprehensions to see the game for what it was—an opportunity to giggle.

The tails in this quilt represent objects we fear. Upon closer examination, the scary objects reveal their true color: pink. How scary could that be?

Getting this quilt from an idea in my head to what you see was quite an adventure. I started with the cats. Their swishing tails look to me like claws when they mirror one another. One of my friends sees swishing tails that get tangled together. I like that.

The number of blocks necessary to fill the center of the quilt was dictated by the gorgeous piece of antique trim with its intricate hand beading that resembles claws. It was a large rectangle that had been taken from an Indian sari. I couldn't cut this handmade treasure! The quilt had to shift and adjust and fit within this piece of trim.

To begin the quilt, I made several cats and liked the way they looked. But I soon began to wonder how many of these could I make and still keep my sanity? The triangles were born to appease my laziness. Luckily for me, the triangles actually work better in the quilt than a sea of cats would have. They add interest and spark imagination.

Besides taking on a new elegant size, the quilt born in fright now elicited giggles. Not only had the scary claws become silly fuchsia tails, but they were encircled by sparkly pink sequins. And thus the long ago memory of a game born of the joy a man took in his infant grandson became CAVE UNGULUM, beware of the claw!

Gathering Your Fabrics

- Triangle background and borders: very light, black-on-off-white print, medium scale, 4¼ yd.
- Cat background: light, black-on-off-white shirting, small scale, 4 yd.
- Cat: black solid, 1 yd.

- Zinger: medium to medium-dark tone-on-tone pink, ½ yd.
- Triangles: medium-dark, gray-on-black print, medium scale, ⅜ yd.
- Multicolor off-white 2¾" trim: 7 yd.
- Backing: 6 yd.
- Batting: 65" x 104"
- Binding (bias cut): ⅞ yd.
- Foundation fabric (12" wide): 15½ yd.

Fabric suggestions

This quilt is about things not being as they seem. That message is carried throughout the fabric choices as well (figs. 1 and 2).

- The choice of a solid black for the cat was almost automatic for me.
- I love using reproduction and vintage fabrics in contemporary quilts. The reproduction shirting I used for the cat background with its old-fashioned timbre starkly contrasts the modern lines of the cat.

- The background for the triangles is flowing and beautiful. It has a slightly lighter value than the shirting, and therefore adds movement to the design.
- The triangle fabric is one that I just adore. It has angles and dots of color and yet maintains a reproduction feel.
- Adding the splash of color on the swisher tails and color border is the perfect spark to liven up the quilt. It pulls out the fabulous color of the sequins in the trim.

Fig. 2. You would think that this antique trim was made for this quilt.

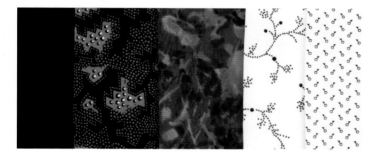

Fig. 1. Something old and something new add flavor to this quilt.

Cutting List All strips are cut across width of fabric unless otherwise stated. Binding strips are cut on the bias.	
Fabric	**Strips (Trim selvages off all strips after first cut.)**
Triangle background and border, 4¼ yd.	two 1¾" for top and bottom partial borders
	two 3" for top and bottom partial borders
	four 3½"
	five 7"
	four 10" x 81½" cut lengthwise for outer border
Cat background, 4 yd.	twelve 2"
	six 2½"
	three 4"
	eight 4¼"
	eight 5¼"
Cat, 1 yd.	six 1¾"
	three 2½"
	four 3"
Triangles. ⅜ yd.	two 4¾" for triangles
Zinger, ½ yd.	two 1¼" for top and bottom partial borders
	six 1¾" for swisher tails
Foundation fabric, 15½ yd.	forty-five squares 12" x 12"

• The trim shown in figure 2 on page 49 was removed from an antique Indian sari. It is a lovely complement to this quilt. Just look at those hand stitched claws!

Preparing the Foundations

1. With a transfer pen, trace one copy of the Triangle block pattern (page 53) onto a sheet of white paper. Add ¼" seam allowances around the outside of the block. Press to transfer the tracing onto 13 foundation squares. If the ink becomes too faint, retrace the existing lines with the transfer pen, and keep going. You can mark the numbers for the cat pieces. The numbers may show through the light background fabrics, so try to do without those numbers on the foundations.

2. Repeat step 1 to trace the Cat block pattern sections (page 52). Add ¼" seam allowances to each foundation section, and transfer them to 32 foundation squares.

Assembling Your Blocks

1. Use the triangle background strips and the 4¾" triangle strips to piece 13 Triangle blocks. Press well and trim each block to an 8" square.

2. For the Cat blocks, you will start with the paws. Sew six strips-sets with one 1¾" black strip and one 1¾" light background strip in each set.

3. Cut 32 pieces from the Left Paw template and 32 pieces from the Right Paw template (fig. 3). Save the scraps for the ears and tails.

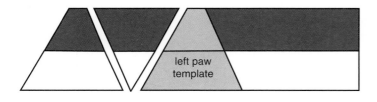

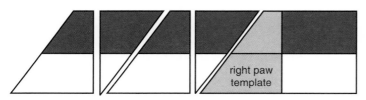

Fig. 3. Cut 32 paws from each template (page 51).

4. Piece the Cat Belly, Left Ear, and Right Ear sections. Use your zinger fabric for the swisher tails in 14 of the cat blocks, and use your cat fabric for the tails in 18 of the blocks. Trim the inside cutting lines only in each section, marked in red in figure 4.

Fig. 4. Cat block assembly

5. Assemble rows of blocks as shown in the quilt assembly diagram on page 51. The strip widths to use for the pieces are shown on the pattern.

Adding the Borders

1. For the top and bottom partial borders, make two strip-sets with one 1¾" light border strip, one 1¼" zinger strip, and one 3" light border strip, as shown in the quilt assembly diagram. Cut a 38" segment from each strip-set, and sew these to the top and bottom of the quilt.

2. For the outer border, cut two 10" x 77" light border strips and sew one to each side of the quilt. Then cut two 10" x 57" strips and sew them to the top and bottom of the quilt.

3. Now you get to add that gorgeous trim you found. If you are going to hand quilt your piece, you could add the trim now. If you are sending the quilt out to be done by machine or by hand, you might want to wait until it is returned to add the trim to the surface

of the quilt. You could also choose to eliminate the trim. When you are ready to add the trim, pin and sew it around the inside edge of the outer border. Depending on the type of ribbon you use, you can miter the corners or make do.

Finishing Touches

- You could make a different number of cats and triangles for your quilt. Maybe you have a spot on your wall that needs these cats. Figure out how big you want your finished project to be and go from there. You can change the number of blocks and the widths of the borders to get the size you

want. Remember that I consider these patterns a starting point, not necessarily an end point.

- I chose a wonderful soft vintage wool plaid for the binding. It adds just enough substance to punctuate the quilt, but doesn't overpower the kitties. It is an off-white with black plaid.
- I quilted two columns of Roman chamomile vines vertically around the central row of Cat blocks. I quilted Roman columns (vertical lines) on each side with arches across the top and bottom to amplify the vertical elegance of the quilt's shape. The cats are reframed in a vine with leaves reminiscent of Caesar's headgear.
- In case you're wondering, we have my friend the Latin teacher to thank for helping me name this quilt.

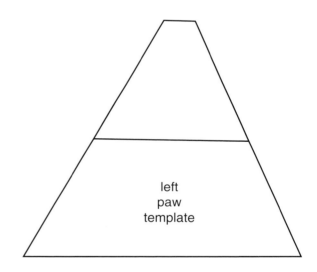

CAVE UNGULUM quilt assembly

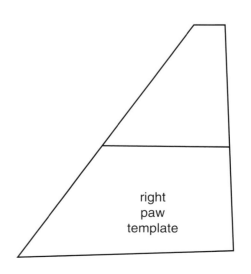

CAT BLOCK

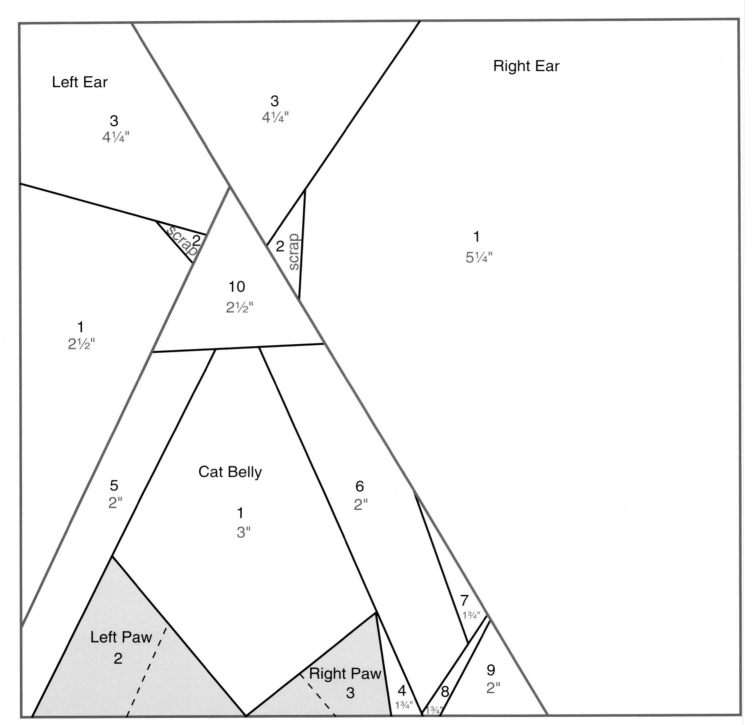

Sections are outlined in red. Add ¼" seam allowance around the outside of the block.

TRIANGLE BLOCK

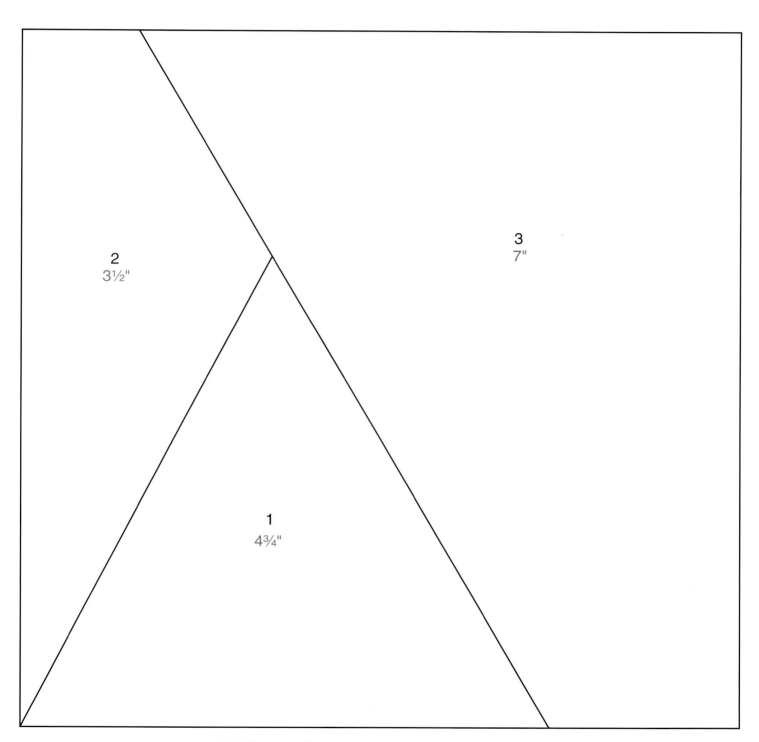

Add ¼" seam allowance around the outside of the block.

No Fences, Please!

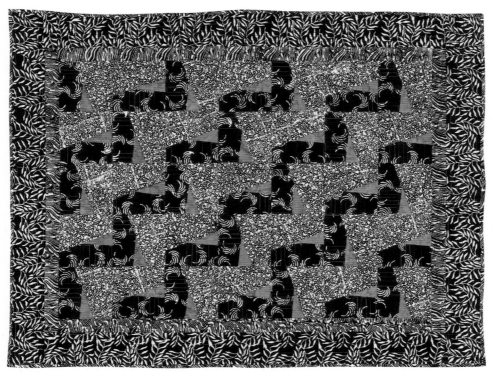

41" x 53" Made by the author.

I really enjoy the simplicity and beauty of traditional quilt blocks. The Rail Fence block has always intrigued me because of its endless possibilities and clean lines. Of course, I couldn't just design a Rail Fence quilt with straight lines and symmetry, that wouldn't be my style. I gave it my own twist and came up with my own fences that celebrate angles and freedom from symmetry.

This quilt represents my sheer joy in simple shapes intermingled with splashes of color. Repetition of one simple block creates the pattern in this quilt. I see fences in my design. Maybe you see other possibilities. It could be that shifting the values or even the position of the zinger in the block will make it look like something else altogether. What would happen if you arranged the blocks differently? Have fun with this quilt. Let your imagination run wild. When it comes to using your imagination, no fences, please!

Gathering Your Fabrics

You will need four fabrics for this quilt. The yardages are based on 42" wide fabric.

- Background: medium-light, black circles on white print, small scale, 1⅛ yd.
- Fences: dark, white-on-black print, large scale, ¾ yd.
- Zinger: intense orange batik, ⅜ yd.
- Inner border and binding: medium-dark, black-on-white zebra print, medium scale, 1 yd.
- Outer border: medium-dark, white-on-black leaf print, large scale, ¾ yd.
- Backing: 2¾ yd.
- Batting: 49" x 61"
- Foundation Fabric (8" wide): 7 yd.

Fabric suggestions

Strong contrasts in value and color will draw your eye to this quilt and not let it go (figs. 1 and 2).

- For the medium and dark fabrics in the blocks, choose pieces with very different scale and value. The movement in the quilt is created by the contrast between these two fabrics.

Fig. 1. Differences in value and scale draw these fabrics together and let them stand apart.

- The zinger should be bold and vibrant. Solids or very saturated tone-on-tones will work well.

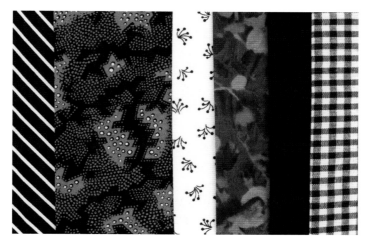

Fig. 2. Try some of the zinger color in the medium-value inner border.

- The outer border can be a repeat of the dark fences fabric in the blocks. Or you could toss in another fabric close in value to the dark. It should be a few shades darker than the inner border to frame the quilt. Play with varying scales to see what you like best.

Piecing and Assembling Your Fences Blocks

1. With a transfer pen, trace one copy of the Fences pattern on page 57. Add ¼" seam allowances to the traced pattern. Press to transfer these onto 35 foundation squares. If the ink begins to fade, retrace the pattern with transfer pen, and continue. You can mark the numbers for the dark fence

pieces. The numbers may show through the light background fabric, so try to do without writing that number on the foundations.

2. Piece 35 Fences blocks. Trim the finished blocks to make 6½" squares (fig. 3).

3. Sew 15 pairs of blocks as shown in figure 3. To position the second block in each pair, rotate it once counterclockwise.

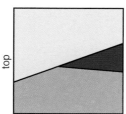
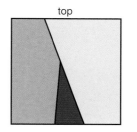

Fig. 3. Sew 15 pairs of blocks.

4. Join three pairs of blocks, then add one block top-side up to the end of the row (fig. 4). Make three of these rows.

Fig. 4. Assemble 3 rows.

5. Join three pairs, then add one block rotated clockwise to the beginning of the row (fig. 5). Make two of these rows.

Fig. 5. Make 2 rows.

Cutting List All strips are cut across width of fabric unless otherwise stated. Binding strips are cut on the bias.

Fabric	Strips (Trim selvages off all strips after first cut.)
Background, 1⅛ yd.	seven 5"
Fences, ¾ yd.	seven 3½"
Zinger, ⅜ yd.	five 2¼"
Inner border, 1 yd.	four 2", save remainder for binding
Outer border, ¾ yd.	five 4½"
Foundation fabric, 7 yd.	thirty-five squares 7" x 7"

6. Assemble your rows according to the quilt assembly diagram.

Adding the Borders

1. For the inner border, join four 2" inner border strips. Cut two 2" x 30½" strips and sew one to each side of the quilt. Then cut two 2" x 45½" strips and sew them to the top and bottom of the quilt.

2. For the outer border, join five 4½" medium-dark strips. Cut two 33½" strips and sew one to each side of the quilt. Then cut two 53½" strips and sew them to the top and bottom of the quilt.

Finishing Touches

- To contrast the angular quality of this quilt, I quilted a circular motif with a variegated thread on the light fabric in the blocks.

- I didn't hold down the zinger with quilting. This boosts the texture and makes the zinger pop even more.

- I accented the strong, straight fence lines by quilting parallel lines on the dark fence fabric.

- Whether you quilt this yourself, or add another dimension to the quilt by having a professional longarm quilter do the handiwork, make sure you add a label or sign the quilt when you are done. Wouldn't it be great to add the machine quilter's signature too?

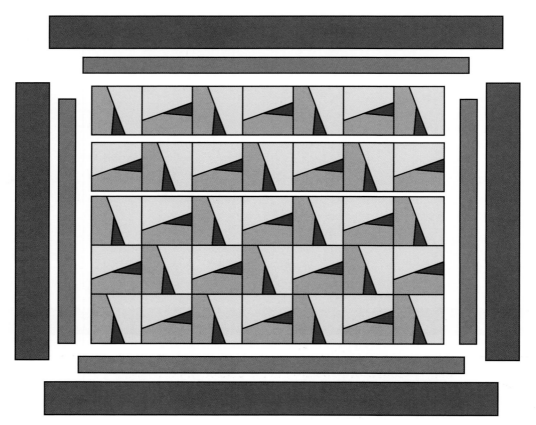

No Fences, Please! quilt assembly

FENCES BLOCK

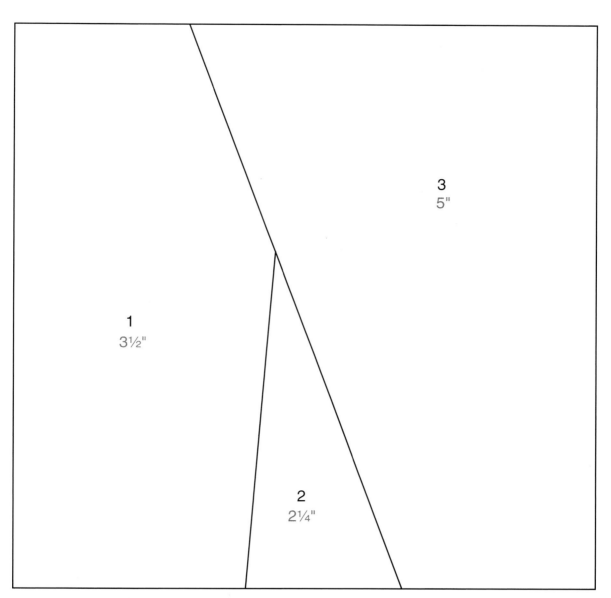

3
5"

1
3½"

2
2¼"

Add ¼" seam allowance around the outside of the block.

DOOR NUMBER ONE

33½" x 50½" Made by the author.

You can tell by my designs that I am very fond of strong lines and the unexpected angle. Aside from their visual impact, each of my designs has a narrative. A thread from my life story is woven into every quilt.

My ideas and my stories spin around inside my head and burst through the surface as quilts. They appear when they want and they tell the story they want. This quilt is about my struggle to see the glass as half full. It has often been easier and more comfortable for me to see the negative side of situations. I have been able to relay a whole list of things that are wrong with a situation, but often, I haven't been able to see a positive side. The more I work on it, I have discovered that it truly improves my life when I see the glass as half full. It makes it easier to navigate through difficulties and glean the lessons from the bumps in my life.

Along with adjusting how I view situations is the notion of opening doors—traveling forward instead of wallowing in the complexities of the past. The doors are filled with movement and possibility. Lurking behind each panel, undiscovered wonders and challenges are waiting to be revealed. The play of the light and dark unknowns intrigue and invite me to choose new doors to open and venture through. In any situation, there is always a choice. For today, I'll take Door Number One.

Gathering Your Fabrics

You will need four fabrics for this quilt. The yardages are based on 42" wide fabric.

- Doors: assorted medium to medium-dark, white-on-black prints, varying scales, 8 different fat quarters
- Light background: light, white-on-white print, ⅝ yd.
- Dark background: outer border and binding (bias cut). Dark, solid, or mottled black, 1⅔ yd.
- Zinger: intense tone-on-tone red, medium to large scale, ¼ yd.
- Lattice: medium-dark, black-on-white coil print, medium scale, ⅓ yd.
- Inner border: medium-dark, white-on-black polka-dot print, small scale, ½ yd.
- Batting: 41" x 58"
- Backing: 1⅞ yd.
- Foundation Fabric (12" wide): 3¼ yd.

Fabric suggestions

Be bold and daring. Go for major differences in scale and value (figs. 1 and 2).

- Use this pattern as an opportunity to play with visual texture created by differences in value and scale.
- For your light background, use a pure white or white-on-white to achieve the greatest contrast with an intense black as its opposite.

Fig 2. Use the brightest zinger you can find.

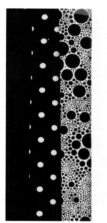

Fig. 1. Use a range of medium-light to medium-dark fabrics.

- By using undiluted blacks and whites in your backgrounds, you can play to your heart's content with a myriad of medium prints for the doors.
- You need the panels in the door to stand out, so having a variety of medium values within the door fabrics is crucial.
- A bright, pure zinger will make the baseboard pop right out.

Piecing Your Door Blocks

1. With a transfer pen, trace one copy of the Door pattern onto a sheet of white paper. Press to transfer the pattern onto 12 foundation squares. If the ink begins to fade, retrace the pattern with transfer pen, and continue. You can mark the numbers for the door pieces. The numbers may show through your light background fabric, so try to do without writing those numbers on the foundations.

2. Cut one each of the 7½" and 3" light background and dark background strips and two of the 1" zinger strips in half to make strips 21" long. Sew one of each strip-set, as shown in figure 3 on page 60. Cut six segments 2¼" from each strip-set. Set these aside for now.

Cutting List All strips are cut across width of fabric unless otherwise stated. Binding strips are cut on the bias.	
Fabric	**Strips (Trim selvages off all strips after first cut.)**
Doors, 8 fat quarters	two 3" x 18" from each fat quarter
Light background, ⅝ yd.	four 3"
	one 7½"
Dark background and outer border, 1⅔ yd.	four 3"
	four 4"
	one 7½"
Lattice, ⅓ yd.	six 1½"
Inner border, ½ yd.	four 2½"
Zinger, ¼ yd.	six 1"
Foundation fabric, 3¼ yd.	twelve rectangles 7" x 10"

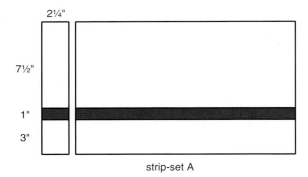

2¼"

7½"

1"

3"

strip-set A

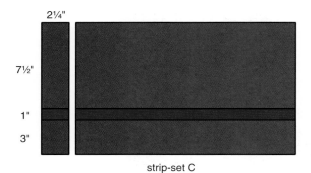

2¼"

7½"

1"

3"

strip-set B

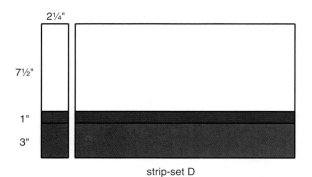

2¼"

7½"

1"

3"

strip-set C

2¼"

7½"

1"

3"

strip-set D

Fig. 3. Cut six segments 2¼" wide from each strip-set.

3. Select a group of three different medium to medium-dark 3" strips for each door. Label the fabrics in

each group, a, b, and c. Vary the value placement from group to group. (fig. 4). For example, in some groups label the lightest fabric with b, in other groups, label the darkest fabric with b. The strip widths to use are shown on the pattern

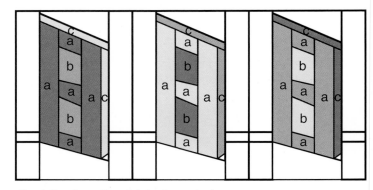

Fig. 4. Use 3 medium fabrics in each door.

4. Piece 6 Door blocks with segments A and B, using the light background fabric for pieces 9 and 12, and the dark background fabric for piece 11 as shown in figure 5. Piece six door blocks with segments C and D, using the dark background fabric for pieces 9 and 12, and the light background fabric for piece 11 (fig. 5).

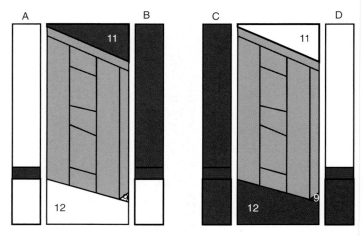

Fig. 5. Assemble 6 of each block.

5. Trim each finished block to 6½" x 9½". Assemble the blocks in *vertical* rows, according the quilt diagram on page 61.

6. Cut four 1½" x 36½" lattice strips. Sew your vertical rows of blocks together beginning and ending with 1 lattice strip. Cut two 1½" x 22½" lattice strips and sew them to the top and bottom of the quilt.

Adding the Borders

1. For the inner border, join four 2½" medium-dark strips. Cut two 2½" x 38½" strips and sew one to each side of the quilt. Then cut two 2½" x 26½" strips and sew them to the top and bottom of the quilt. Cut two 1" x 26½" zinger strips and add them to the top and bottom of the quilt.

2. For the outer border, join four 4" dark background strips. Cut two 4" x 43½" strips and sew one to each side of the quilt. Then cut two 4" x 33½" strips and sew them to the top and bottom of the quilt.

Finishing Touches

- I suggest quilting this piece so that the backgrounds recede and the doors pop out. You could use vertical lines or zigzags or even meandering to pull back the background.
- I used zigzags to contrast what I call licorice quilting in the lattice and inner border.
- The doors don't need much quilting. They can simply be stitched in the ditch and allowed to puff out, or toss in some spirals in the panels.
- Add a hanging sleeve. Then honor your work with a personalized label or at least a date and signature.

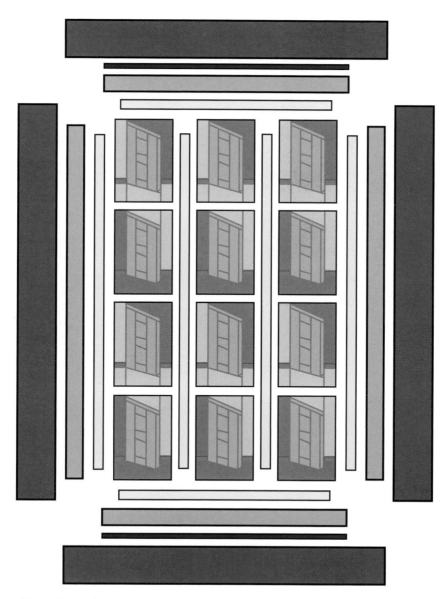

Door Number One quilt assembly

**DOOR NUMBER
ONE BLOCK**

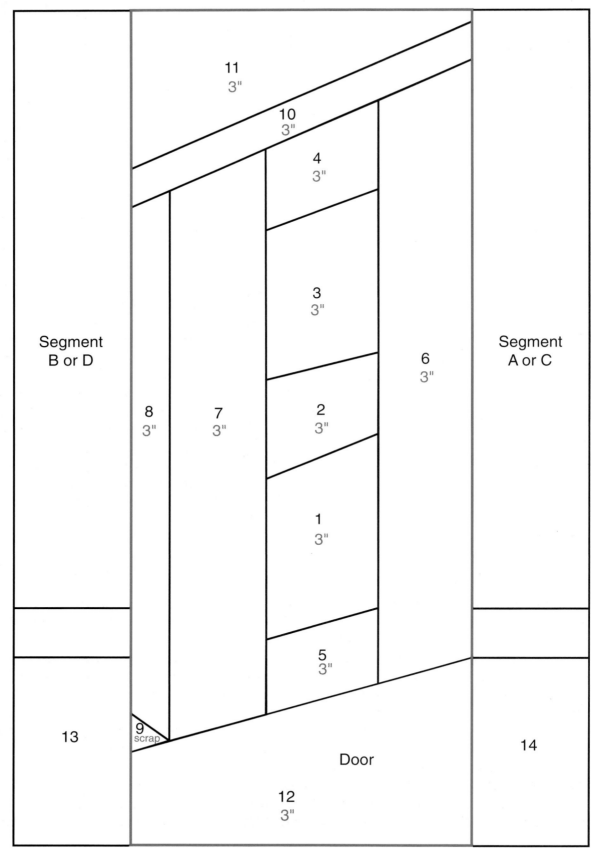

11
3"

10
3"

4
3"

3
3"

Segment
B or D

Segment
A or C

6
3"

8
3"

7
3"

2
3"

1
3"

5
3"

13

9
scrap

14

Door

12
3"

Add ¼" seam allowance around the Door section.

CATWHEELS

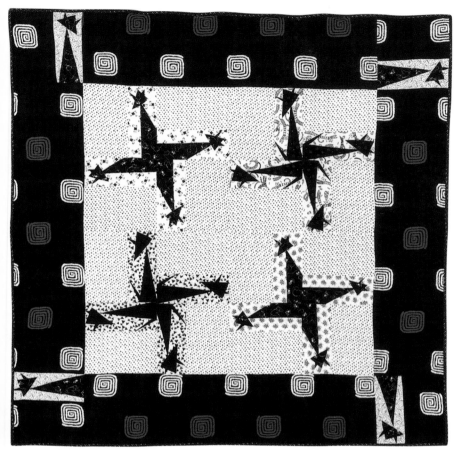

54" x 54" Made by the author.

Three feline beauties, Chloe, Corner, and Clarice share their apartment with Val. They allow her to go out for most of every day while they nap. But her evenings belong to them. She makes her lap available to lounge on and provides their daily quota of stroking—behind their ears and there, no, just there, under their chins. On those rare evenings when she is preoccupied, tending to neglect her duties, they chide Val for her distraction. They expect nothing less than her complete and undivided attention.

One evening Val whirled into the apartment and then spun right past them. No greeting, no pat, not even a passing glance. This would not do. The feline trio tried subtle cajoling first, then blatant demands for her attention. Nothing was working.

Val was on a mission that they didn't understand. She was not reaching for her sweats. What is that little black dress for? Coiled around her ankles, their twisting bodies didn't even break her stride as Val raced to her closet. The drone of their imploring purrs fell on deaf ears. Rolling onto their backs, paws cutely curled didn't even merit Val's notice.

Now Val had shut herself in the bathroom and was taking a shower. But it wasn't morning. Something was definitely wrong. Corner was completely confused. Unable to sort this crisis out, she streaked to her corner and sat still as a stone. Not ones to sulk, Chloe and Clarice pounced into action, twisting and turning with yowling to accompany their gyrations. Val emerged. Perhaps she had heard them. No. She was freshly painted, dressed, and heading for the door.

"Meeooow!" the duo screeched, and frantically resumed their feline gymnastics. Clarice daringly vaulted from the back of the couch to attack Val's feet. They had done everything they could to get her attention. There was only one trick left. It was their show stopper—Catwheels.

Gathering Your Fabrics

The yardages are based on 42" wide fabric.

- Cat background: assorted light, black-on-off-white prints, medium-scale, 1¼ yd. total
- Left-side background: light, black on off-white, small-scale print, ¾ yd.
- Cats: assorted dark, white-on-black prints, small-scale, 1 yd. total
- Border: dark, black-and-multicolor print, large-scale, 1¾ yd.
- Backing: 3⅜ yd.
- Batting: 62" x 62"
- Binding (bias cut): ¾ yd.
- Foundation fabric: (12" wide) 7 yd.

Fabric suggestions

You will need four fabrics for this quilt (figs. 1 and 2).

- The background and the left-side background should have a subtle difference in their values. The slight variation pops the kitties' auras right out.
- You can use a variety of prints for the cats. Just make sure their value is very dark and they all read about the same. Play with the scale of prints to add variety.

Fig. 1. Use a slight difference in value and scale to make the light fabrics stand out from each other.

- Use a very dramatic fabric for the border. This design is simple and a powerful border will make this quilt soar.

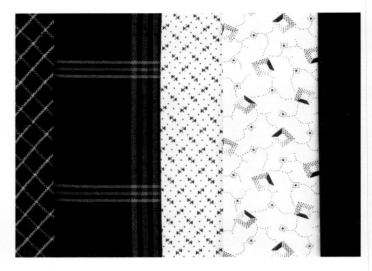

Fig. 2. Go for a dramatic border fabric.

Piecing Your Cat Blocks

1. With a transfer pen, trace one copy of the pattern sections for Chloe, Corner, and Clarice (pages 67–69) onto sheets of white paper. You can mark the numbers for the cat pieces. The numbers may show through the light background fabrics, so try to do it without writing those numbers on the foundations. Add ¼" seam allowances around each foundation section.

2. Press to transfer the sections for one cat onto one foundation square. Make eight copies each of Clarice and Chloe, and four copies of Corner. This will give you foundation patterns for 20 cat blocks.

Cutting List
All strips are cut across width of fabric unless otherwise stated. Binding strips are cut on the bias.

Fabric	Strips (Trim selvages off all strips after first cut.)
Cat background, 1¼ yd.	nine 2½"
	six 3"
Left-side background, ¾ yd.	sixteen rectangles 6" x 9½"
Cats, 1 yd.	four 3"
	four 4"
Border, 1¾ yd.	four lengthwise 9½" strips (Trim selvages off before cutting strips.)
	four rectangles 6" x 9½"
Foundation fabric, 7 yd.	20 squares 12" x 12"

3. Use the black cat and the cat background fabrics to piece each cat. The strip widths to use for the pieces are shown on the patterns. Trim the cat sections around their cutting lines and assemble them according to the diagrams in figures 3 a–c.

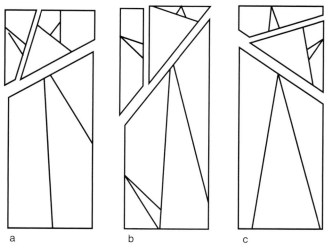

Fig. 3. (a) Chloe block assembly, (b) Clarice block assembly, (c) Corner block assembly

4. Trim each cat block to 4" x 9½". Sew a 6" x 9½" left-side background piece to each Chloe and Clarice block (fig. 4). Sew the 6" x 9½" border-fabric rectangles to Corner's block.

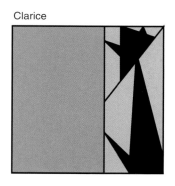

Clarice

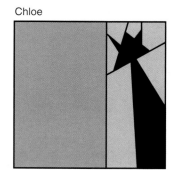

Chloe

Fig. 4. Add background pieces.

5. Sew two Chloe blocks together, rotating the second block clockwise one turn (fig. 5). Make four of these.

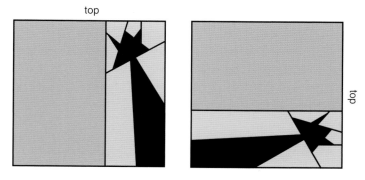

top

Fig. 5. Assemble two for each Cat block.

6. Join two pairs of Chloe blocks to assemble a Cat-wheel block, rotating the lower block two clockwise turns (fig 6). Make two of these.

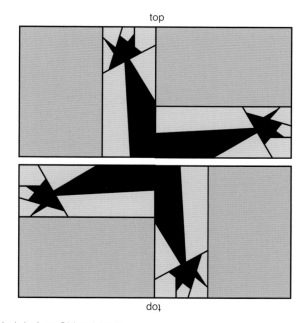

top

doʇ

Fig. 6. Join four Chloe blocks.

7. Repeat steps 5 and 6 to make two Clarice Catwheel blocks.
8. Join the Chloe and Clarice Catwheels catty-corner in two rows, as shown in the quilt assembly diagram, on page 66.
9. For the border, cut two 9½" x 36½" strips and sew one to each side of the quilt. Then cut two 9½" x 36½" strips. Add one Corner block to each end of the strips, rotating the blocks as shown in the

assembly diagram, and sew them to the top and bottom of the quilt.

Finishing Touches

- This quilt has wonderful open spaces to showcase your hand or machine quilting skills.
- I can see feathered wreaths in the center or a wreath of mice, perhaps?

- I let the fabric do the talking on my quilt. The border fabric is so dramatic, that I didn't want to detract or diminish its singular beauty.
- As always, the right way to quilt it is the way that pleases you.
- Don't forget to date and sign your work! If you have personalized labels, that's great. Attach one and make life easy for future generations of quilt sleuths.

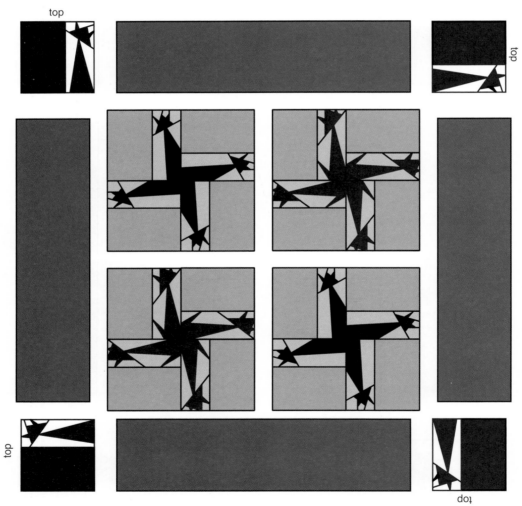

CATWHEELS quilt assembly

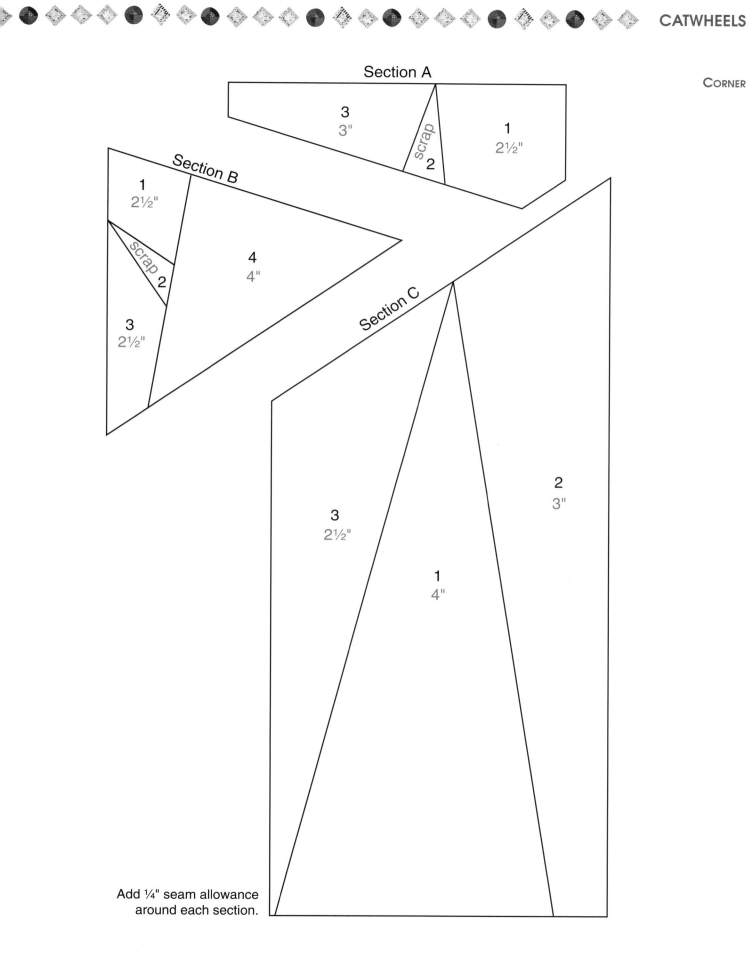

Section A

3
3"

scrap

2

1
2½"

Section B

1
2½"

scrap

2

4
4"

3
2½"

Section C

2
3"

3
2½"

1
4"

Add ¼" seam allowance
around each section.

CHLOE

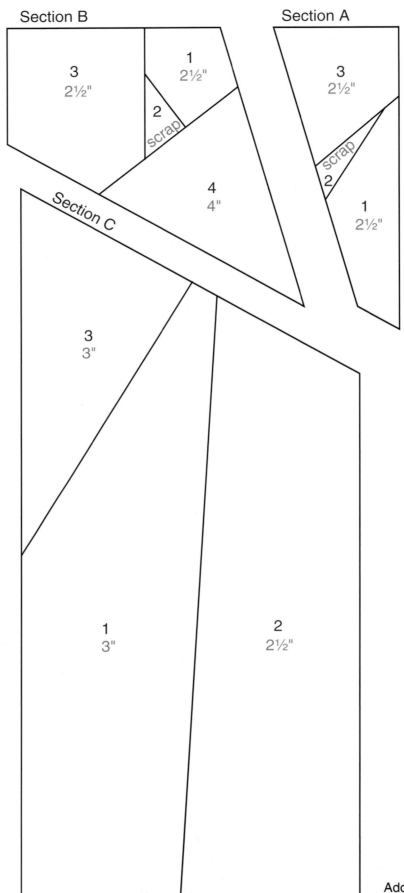

Section B

Section A

3
2½"

1
2½"

2

scrap

Section C

4
4"

3
2½"

scrap

2

1
2½"

3
3"

1
3"

2
2½"

Add ¼" seam allowance
around each section.

Clarice

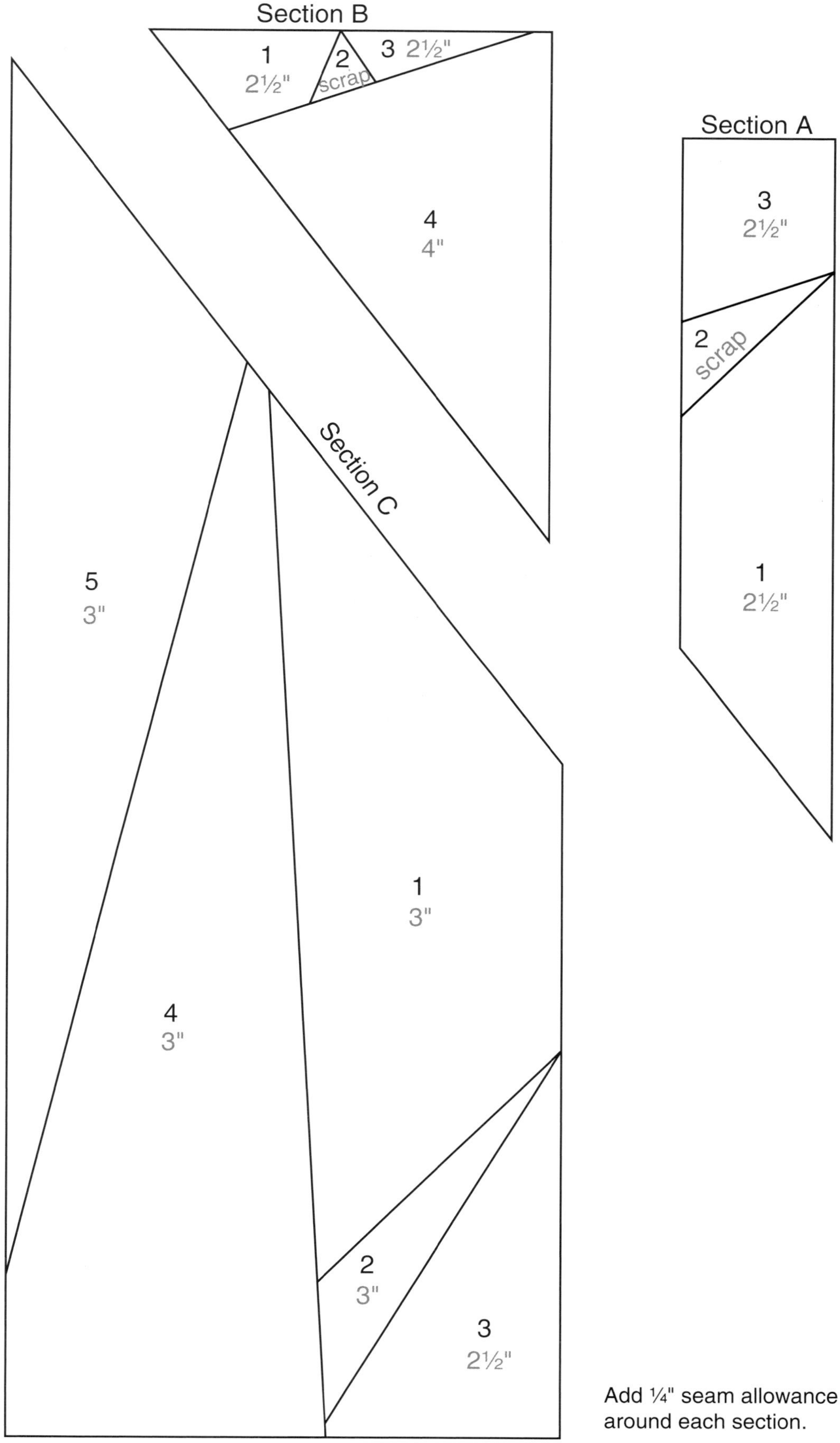

Section B

1
2½"

2
scrap

3 2½"

4
4"

Section A

3
2½"

2 scrap

1
2½"

Section C

5
3"

4
3"

1
3"

2
3"

3
2½"

Add ¼" seam allowance
around each section.

THIS SCHOOL HOUSE ROCKS!

28" x 31" Made by the author.

There is such charm in the simple shape and design of a one-room schoolhouse. The concept of the one room has always intrigued me. I'm sure I would have enjoyed learning in that environment. The camaraderie and inherent competition would make inspiring educational experiences that would be hard to duplicate. The natural challenge would have provided rich and rewarding practice in developing life skills.

My mother and my grandmother both taught in one-room schoolhouses. My mom taught at the same school that she attended as a child. What a wonderful link in history. The lovely little schoolhouses left a strong legacy. The heritage we cherish is not confined to the charming structures left behind, but includes the strong belief in the three Rs as a solid base for living a productive, connected, and charitable life in society.

- Background: light, black-on-off-white shirting, small scale, ¾ yd.
- Schoolhouse: dark, white-on-black chalkboard print, medium scale, ¼ yd.
- School bell and door: medium, red circles on off-white, medium scale, ⅛ yd.
- Door frame and roof: medium, black-and-white gingham check, small scale, ⅛ yd.
- Blades of grass and bell clapper: medium, red print, small scale. Scraps, 1 fat eighth total
- Grass (foundation piece 7): medium-light, multicolor with dashes of red floral print, medium scale, ⅛ yd.
- Middle ground (foundation piece 9) and windows: medium-light, black-on-off-white floral print, medium-scale, ⅛ yd.
- Bottom ground (foundation piece 11): medium, black-and-white gingham check, large scale, ¼ yd.
- Zinger for flat-piping border: red tone-on-tone print, ¼ yd.
- Inner border: medium-light, black-on-off-white geometric print, medium scale, ¼ yd.
- Medium-dark outer border: medium dark, off-white-on-black cobweb print, large scale ⅜ yd.
- Dark outer border: dark, off-white squiggles on black print, medium scale ⅜ yd.
- Backing: 1 yd.
- Batting: 36" x 39"
- Binding (bias cut): ½ yd.
- Foundation fabric (20" wide): 1 yd.

Fabric suggestions

You only need small amounts of each fabric, so have fun raiding your stash for this quilt (fig. 1, page 71).

- Choose fabrics with very strong contrast for the background and the schoolhouse. There is a lot going on with the fabrics in this piece, so you want to make sure that the schoolhouse stands out forcefully against the background.

- Have a lot of fun with fabrics for the accent shapes. The door and roof work well as a gingham check, plaid, strong geometric, or graphic print. Play with the windows. Is someone peeking out? The school bell was a central part of the school day. Use a print that celebrates its importance.

- The color shapes are few, but important in this

Fig. 1. Keep an eye on the values and scales of your fabrics, then anything goes.

piece. I used a vintage gingham print for the door frame and roof. The grass and grass blades are vintage red prints that I had in a scrap bag. It pays to save those scraps.

- The ground and middle ground fabrics should be coordinating prints that add to the playful quality of the quilt. I used different scales to add texture and interest.

- The zinger border fabric should be bold, but not overpowering. This quilt's story is in the center, not in the border.

- The outer border fabrics can be repeats of fabrics already in the schoolhouse or they can be new prints. Choose prints very close in value and slightly different in scale. The left and bottom borders should be the darker of the two fabrics. This naturally frames the quilt without distracting your eye from the schoolhouse.

- The inner border works well if it is a tad bit lighter than the outer border and perhaps a slightly different scale. Keeping the value and scale fairly close together in the border will frame the piece and not compete with the center story.

- Finish the piece with a whimsical binding. This isn't a serious piece, so don't worry about treating it like it is. Entertain yourself and your viewers!

Cutting List All strips are cut across width of fabric unless otherwise stated. Binding strips are cut on the bias.

Fabric	Strips (Trim selvages off all strips after cutting.)
Background, ¾ yd.	one 4"
	one 6½"
	one 9½"
Schoolhouse, ¼ yd.	one 2½"
	one 4½"
School bell and door, ⅛ yd.	one 2½" for door and school bell
Door frame and roof, ⅛ yd.	one 1¼" for door frame
	one 2¼" for roof
Grass blades and bell clapper, 1 fat eighth	one 1"
	one 1" square for clapper
Grass, ⅛ yd.	one 2¾" for grass
Middle ground and windows, ⅛ yd.	one 3½" for middle ground and windows
Bottom ground, ¼ yd.	one 4"
Zinger piping border, ¼ yd.	three 1¼"
Inner border, ¼ yd.	three 1¾"
Medium-dark outer border, ⅜ yd.	two 5½"
Dark outer border, ⅜ yd.	two 5½"
Foundation fabric, 1 yd.	one piece 17" x 20"
	two 7" x 20"

Piecing Your School House

1. Make a 150% enlargement of the pattern on pages 76 and 77. Outline a 15½" x 18½" rectangle onto the 17" x 20" foundation fabric. Trace pieces 2–11 of the School House pattern on pages 76 and 77 onto the foundation fabric. Trace the patterns for the School House sections A–D, page 74, onto the 7" foundation strips. Trace the template for piece 2 onto a sheet of white paper. Add ¼" seam allowances around each section and around the template.

2. Piece School House sections A–C.

3. Sew pieces 1–5 to the section D foundation. The strip widths to use for each piece are shown on the patterns.

4. To make the bell clapper for section D fold the 1" square as shown in figure 2 to make a tiny ¼" square. Press after each fold to make very sharp creases. Pin the square over piece 3 with its raw edges overlapping the seam line for piece 6 (fig. 3). Add piece 6 to the foundation, making sure to catch the corner of the clapper in the seam. Add piece 7 to finish the section.

5. Sew sections A–D together in alphabetical order according to the assembly diagram in figure 4. Use the assembled sections as foundation piece 1. This will create two thicknesses of foundation fabric in your quilt, which adds a little volume to the front of the school house.

6. Cut piece 2 from your paper template. Finish piecing the rest of the quilt. Trim it to a rectangle 16" x 19".

Adding the Borders

1. For the inner border, join three 1¾" strips. Cut two 1¾" x 19" strips from the inner border fabric, and sew one to each side of the quilt, according to the quilt assembly diagram on page 73. Then cut two 1¾" x 18½" strips and sew them to the top and bottom of the quilt. Press the seam allowances toward the border.

2. The zinger border is sewn in as a flat piping (fig. 5, page 73). Cut two 1¼" x 21½" strips from the zinger fabric. Fold the strips in half wrong-sides together, press them, and sew one to each side of the quilt with a ⅛" seam allowance. Leave these strips in place as they are and do not press.

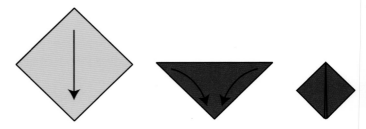

Fig. 2. Three folds give you a tiny square for the clapper.

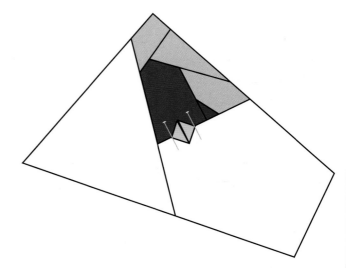

Fig. 3. Pin the clapper to piece 3 so its raw edges will be caught in the seam with piece 6.

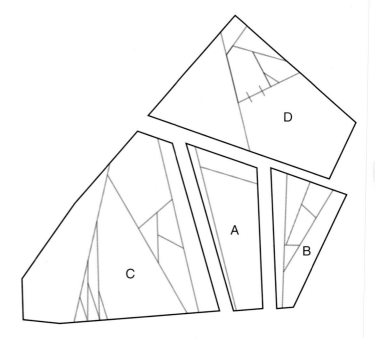

Fig. 4. School House section assembly

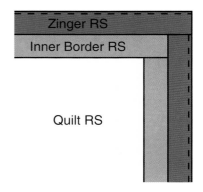

Fig. 5. Zinger piping border

3. Cut two 1¾" x 18½" strips. Fold the strips in half wrong-sides together, and sew them to the top and bottom of the quilt with a ⅛" seam allowance (fig. 6). Leave these in place as they are and do not press.

Zinger RS

Inner Border RS

Quilt RS

Fig. 6. Overlap the folded zinger strips at the corners, and sew with a ⅛ seam allowance.

4. Sew the outer border strips to the quilt with ¼" seams as though the zinger piping strips were not there. Cut one 5½" x 21½" strip from the dark border fabric. Sew this to the left side of the quilt. Cut one 5½" x 21½" from the medium-dark border fabric and sew it to the right side of the quilt. Cut one strip 5½" x 28½" from the dark border fabric and sew it to the bottom of the quilt. Cut one 5½" x 28½" strip from the medium-dark border fabric and sew it to

the top of the quilt. Press the seams toward the outer border being careful not to disturb the piping border.

Finishing Touches

- With so much going in terms of fabric in these designs, I went simple with the quilting.
- I used one of my favorite quilting designs, the zigzag, in the grass.
- I did vertical and horizontal quilting lines in the outer border.
- I did the licorice stitch in the inner border, and then you can see the zigzag echoing the grass above that. It adds nice contrast to oscillate from curves to angles.
- Celebrate your quilt with the label.

THIS SCHOOL HOUSE ROCKS! quilt assembly

THIS SCHOOL HOUSE ROCKS! sections

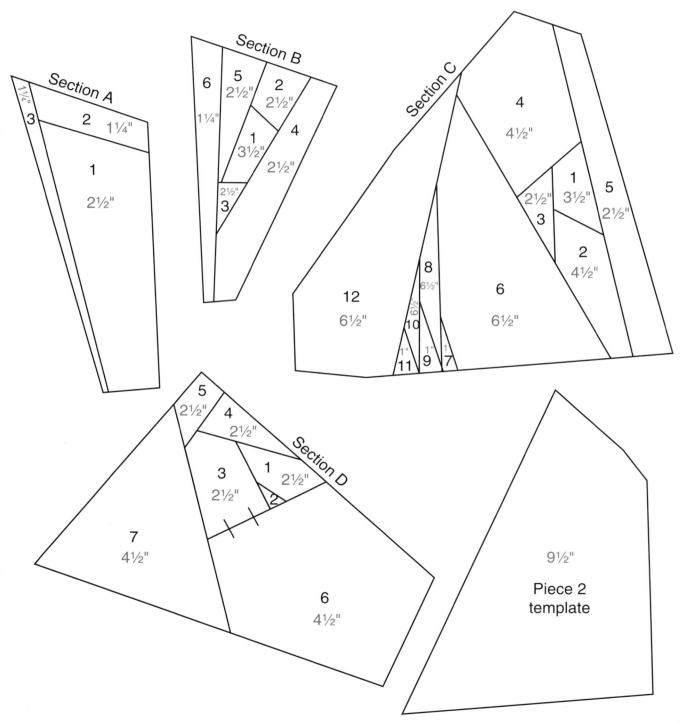

Section A

3 2 1¼"
1¼"

1
2½"

Section B

6 5 2
2½" 2½"
1¼"
1
3½" 4
2½"
2½"
3

Section C

4
4½"

1
2½" 3½" 5
3 2½"
2
4½"

12
6½"

8
6½"
6
6½"
10
6½"
1" 1" 1"
11 9 7

Section D

5
2½"
4
2½"
1
2½"
3
2½"
2

7
4½"

6
4½"

9½"

Piece 2
template

Add ¼" seam allowances around each section and around the template.

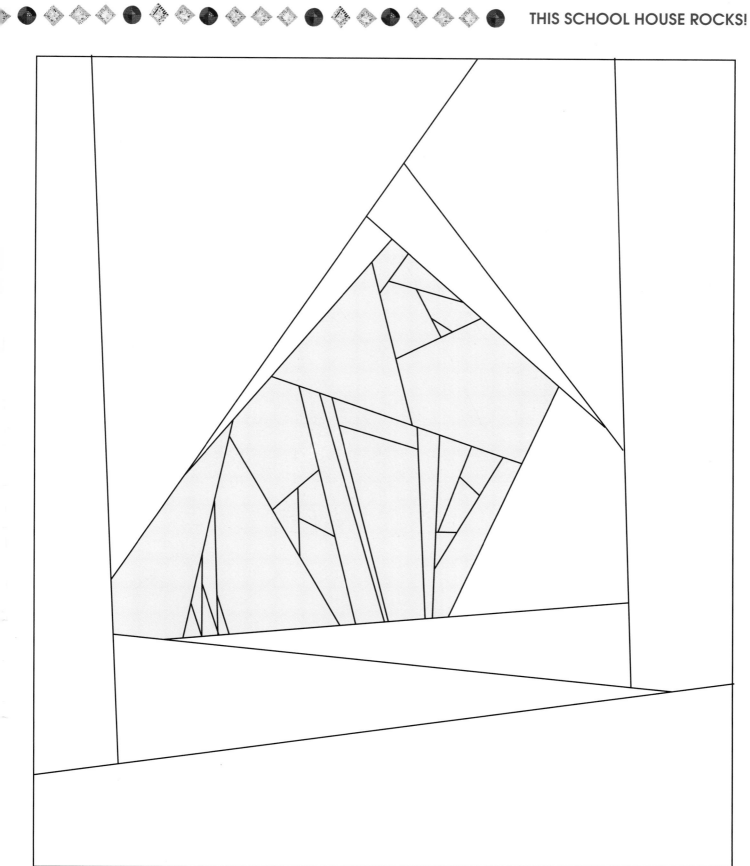

This SCHOOL HOUSE ROCKS! foundation

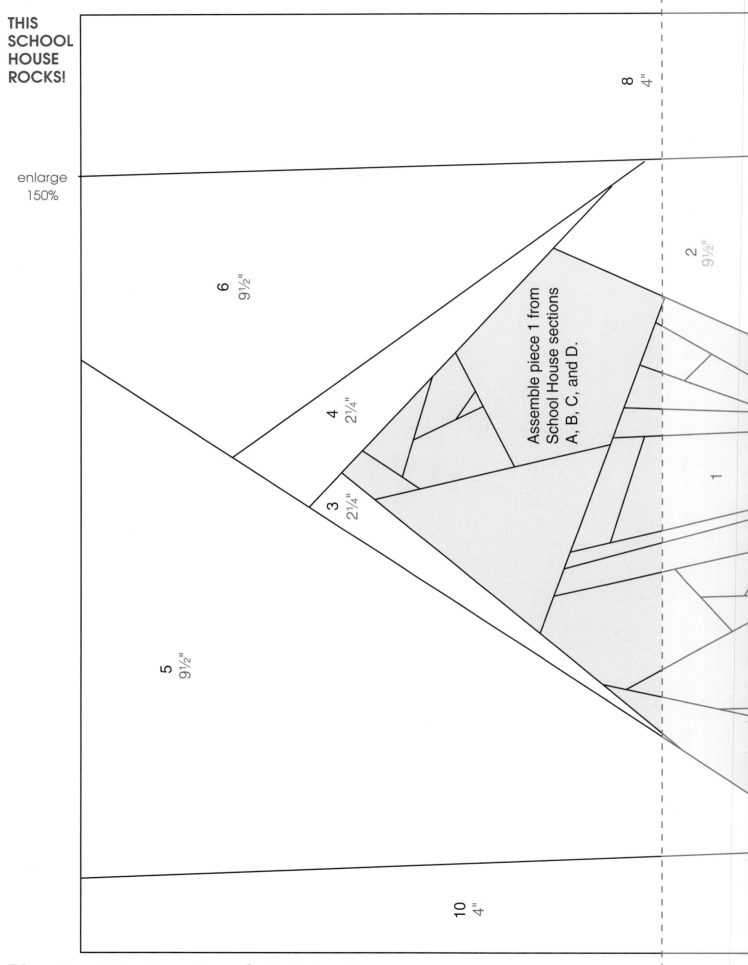

THIS
SCHOOL
HOUSE
ROCKS!

enlarge
150%

8
4"

2
9½"

6
9½"

4
2¼"

3
2¼"

Assemble piece 1 from
School House sections
A, B, C, and D.

1

5
9½"

10
4"

enlarge
150%

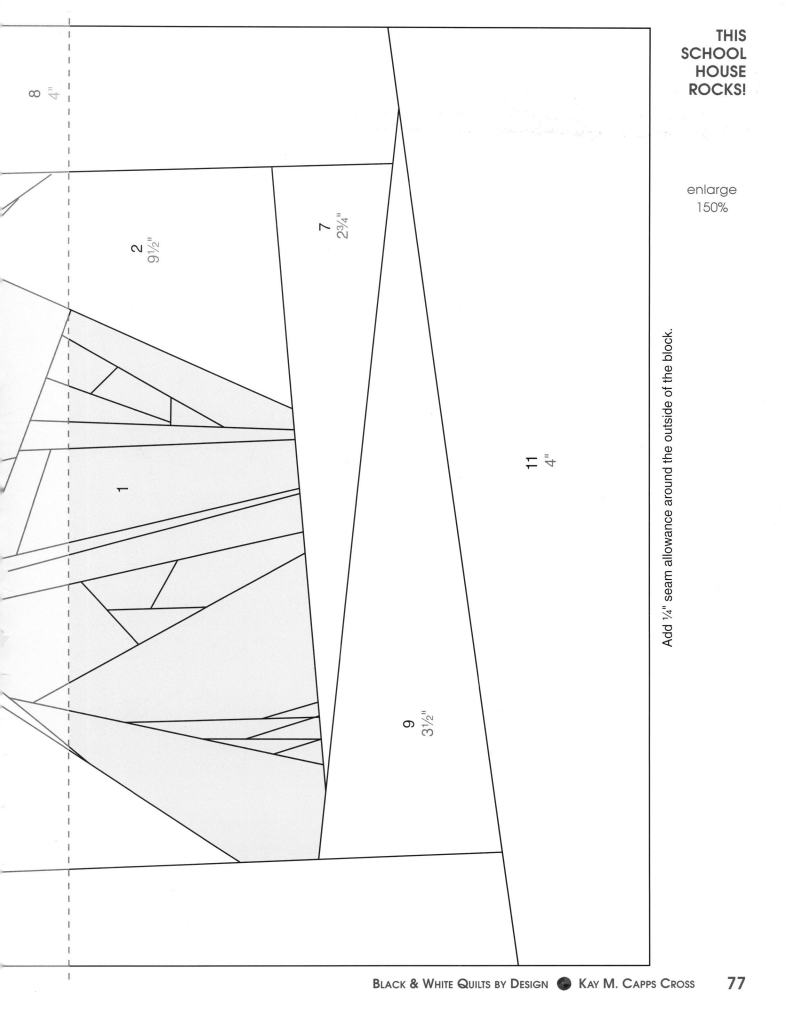

8
4"

2
9½"

7
2¾"

11
4"

1

9
3½"

Add ¼" seam allowance around the outside of the block.

RESOURCES

Fabric

Always check at your local quilt shop first. If you like having them in town, the way to keep them in business is to shop there.

Yellow Bird Art
201 Main Street, Lansing, Iowa 52151
563-538-4350
www.yellowbirdart.com

Big Horn Quilts
529 Greybull Avenue, PO Box 566
Greybull, WY 82426
877-586-9150
outside the US 307-765-2604
www.bighornquilts.com

The Tattered Rabbit Quilt Shop
1660 Hamner Ave. Suite 16
Norco, CA 92860
951-278-9108
www.tatteredrabbit.com

Quilters Round-up
288 N Main St
Heppner, OR 97836
541-676-8282
www.quiltersroundup.com

The Stitch-N-Frame Shop
2222 S Frontage Rd, Suite D
Vicksburg, MS 39180
601-634-0243
www.stitch-n-frame.net

Fabric Shack Stores
99 South Marvin Lane
Waynesville, Ohio 45068
513-897-0092
www.fabricshack.com

E-quilter online catalog
www.equilter.com

Wholesale Suppliers

The author would like to thank the following resources for providing fabrics for this book.

Supplies

Sulky of America
PO Box 494129
Port Charlotte, FL 33949
941/629-3199 Fax: 941/743-4634
(Iron-on Transfer Pen, and Soft 'n Sheer non-woven stabilizer)
www.sulky.com

Fabric

Island Batik, Inc.
1341 Distribution Way #12
Vista, CA 92083
760/599-8724 Fax: 760/599-4751
www.islandbatik.com
(NO FENCES PLEASE!)

Quilting Treasures by Cranston
469 Seventh Avenue
New York, NY 10018
212/244-0794 Fax: 212/946-2345
www.quiltingtreasures.com
(FOOLS TRAVEL IN 4-PACKS)

Red Rooster Fabrics
1359 Broadway, Suite 1202
New York, NY 10019
212/244-6596 Fax: 212/760-1536
(DOOR NUMBER ONE)